P9-DOA-119

DATE DUE

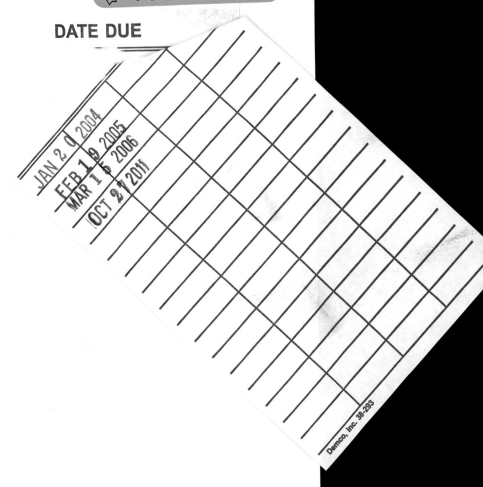

JAN 2 0 2004
FEB 1 9 2005
MAR 1 5 2006
OCT 2 7 2011

Demco, Inc. 38-293

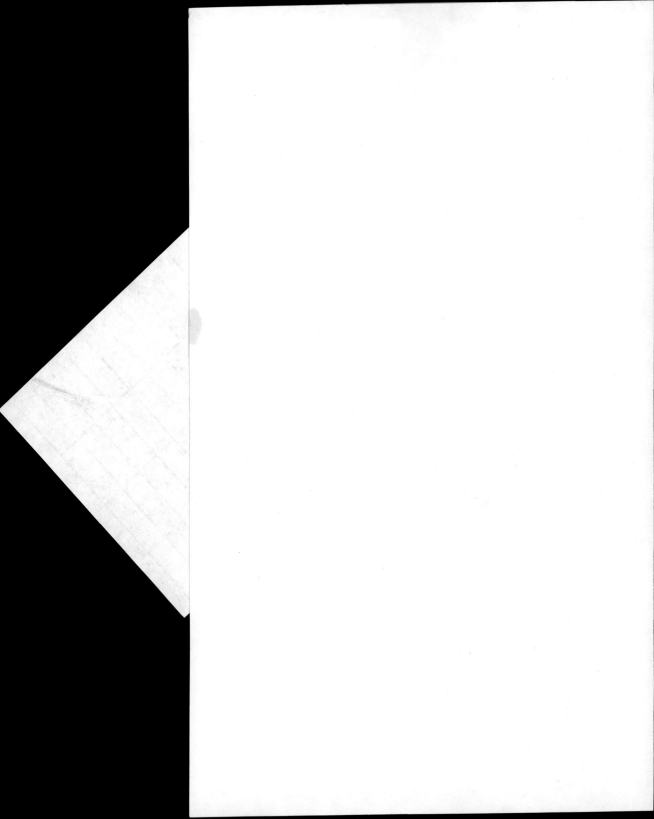

Alien Abductions

Fact or Fiction?

Tamara L. Roleff, *Book Editor*

Daniel Leone, *President*

Bonnie Szumski, *Publisher*

Scott Barbour, *Managing Editor*

OPPOSING
VIEWPOINTS®
SERIES

GREENHAVEN
PRESS®

THOMSON
———✳———™
GALE

San Diego • Detroit • New York • San Francisco • Cleveland
New Haven, Conn. • Waterville, Maine • London • Munich

THOMSON

✱

™

GALE

LIBRARY OF CONGRESS CATALOGING-IN-PUBLICATION DATA

Alien abductions / Tamara L. Roleff, book editor.
  p. cm. — (Fact or fiction?)
Includes bibliographical references and index.
ISBN 0-7377-1589-8 (alk. paper) — ISBN 0-7377-1590-1 (pbk. : alk. paper)
  1. Alien abduction. [1. Alien abduction. 2. Human-alien encounters.
3. Extraterrestrial beings. 4. Unidentified flying objects.] I. Roleff, Tamara L.,
1959– . II. Fact or fiction? (Greenhaven Press)
BF2050 .A34   2003
001.942—dc21
                                                                    2002029937

Contents

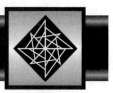

Foreword

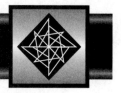

"There are more things in heaven and earth, Horatio, than are dreamt of in your philosophy."
—William Shakespeare, *Hamlet*

"Extraordinary claims require extraordinary evidence."
—Carl Sagan, *The Demon-Haunted World*

Almost every one of us has experienced something that we thought seemed mysterious and unexplainable. For example, have you ever known that someone was going to call you just before the phone rang? Or perhaps you have had a dream about something that later came true. Some people think these occurrences are signs of the paranormal. Others explain them as merely coincidence.

As the examples above show, mysteries of the paranormal ("beyond the normal") are common. For example, most towns have at least one place where inhabitants believe ghosts live. People report seeing strange lights in the sky that they believe are the spaceships of visitors from other planets. And scientists have been working for decades to discover the truth about sightings of mysterious creatures like Bigfoot and the Loch Ness monster.

There are also mysteries of magic and miracles. The two often share a connection. Many forms of magical belief are tied to religious belief. For example, many of the rituals and beliefs of the voodoo religion are viewed by outsiders as magical practices. These include such things as the alleged Haitian voodoo practice of turning people into zombies (the walking dead).

There are mysteries of history—events and places that have been recorded in history but that we still have questions about today. For example, was the great King Arthur a real king or merely a legend? How, exactly, were the pyramids built? Historians continue to seek the answers to these questions.

Then, of course, there are mysteries of science. One such mystery is how humanity began. Although most scientists agree that it was through the long, slow process of evolution, not all scientists agree that indisputable proof has been found.

Subjects like these are fascinating, in part because we do not know the whole truth about them. They are mysteries. And they are controversial—people hold very strong and opposing views about them.

How we go about sifting through information on such topics is the subject of every book in the Greenhaven Press series Fact or Fiction? Each anthology includes articles that present the main ideas favoring and challenging a given topic. The editor collects such material from a variety of sources, including scientific research, eyewitness accounts, and government reports. In addition, a final chapter gives readers tools to analyze the articles they read. With these tools, readers can sift through the information presented in the articles by applying the methods of hypothetical reasoning. Examining these topics in this way adds a unique aspect to the Fact or Fiction? series. Hypothetical reasoning can be applied to any topic to allow a reader to become more analytical about the material he or she encounters. While such reasoning may not solve the mystery of who is right or who is wrong, it can help the reader separate valid from invalid evidence relating to all topics and can be especially helpful in analyzing material where people disagree.

Introduction

People have always looked at the stars and wondered if life existed on other planets. Several ancient cultures tell stories in which beings from the stars visit the earth. Not until the mid–twentieth century, however, did the phenomena of alien abduction become a part of American culture.

Public Opinion

Following the claim of the UFO crash in Roswell, New Mexico, an August 1947 Gallup poll found that of the 90 percent of Americans surveyed who had heard about the UFO crash, less than 1 percent believed that alien visitors were responsible for the crash. A few years later, a 1950 survey by *Public Opinion Quarterly* found that 94 percent of Americans had heard of flying saucers, but only 5 percent actually believed the unidentified flying objects were actually from another planet. Yet after Roswell, the number of flying saucer reports skyrocketed. Some people even claimed they had had contact with the aliens flying the spaceships. The contactees' early reports of meetings with the aliens were similar in many ways. The aliens were benevolent beings who came to Earth to warn humans of the dangers of nuclear and conventional warfare or to share breakthrough technologies and help humankind in other ways. One contactee, George Adamski, even claimed to have made friends with the "Brothers"—extraterrestrial beings—including Orthon from Venus, Firkon from Mars, and Ramu from Saturn. According to Adamski, the Brothers regularly took him aboard their spaceships and flew him to their planets, trips that he described in several books. Detractors claimed that Adamski's descriptions of life on Venus, Mars, and Saturn were contradicted by scientific evidence. Because of the obvious falseness of his claims, most UFO researchers tended to distance themselves from early reports of contact with aliens, and ufology was not taken seriously by many in the scientific and academic communities. Then, in the early 1960s, the credibility of ufology suffered another blow when people began claiming that aliens were abducting them and performing medical and surgical experiments on them. Even some ufologists believed the claims were too bizarre to be believable.

Too Lurid to Publicize

The first modern claim of alien abduction was by Antonio Villas-Boas in Brazil during the late 1950s. According to Villas-Boas, a law student, he was plowing his family's fields one evening when a UFO landed near him. He told researchers that he was immediately carried aboard the spaceship, where he was unclothed, examined, and had blood drawn. Then, a beautiful and curvaceous alien, who looked partly human, entered the room and Villas-Boas was forced to have sex with her. Villas-Boas said he received the impression from her that the aliens were using him like a "stallion to improve their stock."[1] Ufologists suppressed his story until the mid-1960s, fearing it was too sensational and lurid for the American public.

The Hill Case

The first alien abduction story to be widely publicized was that of Barney and Betty Hill, an interracial couple who were widely acknowledged to be solid citizens with no reason to lie about their experience. Barney Hill worked for the Boston post office; Betty Hill was a social worker for the state of New Hampshire. They were both active in the civil rights movement and were devout members of their church.

On September 19, 1961, they were driving through a national forest in New Hampshire late at night when they said they stopped to get a better look at a UFO that seemed to be following them. The second time they stopped, Barney Hill got out of the car. He used his binoculars to see inside the spaceship. He said he saw "many figures scurrying about as though they were making some hurried type of preparation. One figure was observing us from the window." Hill was frightened, thinking they meant to capture him "like a bug in a net,"[2] and he ran back to the car. The Hills drove about thirty miles before Barney Hill inexplicably drove onto an unused dirt road into deep woods and then stopped the car.

When the Hills finally returned home to Portsmouth, New Hampshire, it was almost dawn. Their four-hour trip had taken almost seven hours. The Hills had only vague memories of what had happened to them from the time they drove onto the dirt road in the forest, but they believed they had been abducted by aliens. Betty Hill was convinced she had seen an extraterrestrial spaceship.

After their car stopped on the road in the woods, they remembered being surrounded by strange gray men about five feet tall with black hair and black eyes. The men took them to a metallic disk-shaped craft and led them to different rooms. Inside her room, Betty said a "doctor" performed some tests on her, including a pregnancy test in which he inserted a needle into her abdomen. Barney believed that the aliens had taken a sperm sample from him with a suction device placed on his groin.

Once home, Barney noticed that the strap holding his binoculars was broken, and Betty discovered a strange pink powder on her dress. Barney's groin area was so painful that he examined it in a mirror.

The Hills were deeply affected by their experience. Betty Hill endured six straight nights of terrifying nightmares, which refused to leave her consciousness during the day. The day after their encounter they called nearby Pease Air Force Base to report seeing an unidentified flying object; their call was forwarded to Project Blue Book, the U.S. Air Force's investigating group that collected and examined UFO sightings. The Hills related what little they could remember about their experience. The U.S. Air Force eventually dismissed the object the Hills saw as probably a sighting of the planet Jupiter. Betty Hill also contacted the National Investigations Committee on Aerial Phenomena (NICAP) and reported their strange adventure. They also talked about their UFO sighting with members of their church and with UFO groups.

Barney Hill began feeling stress and depression. About six months after their ordeal, Barney developed warts in a perfect circle around his genitals. He had the warts surgically removed. Finally, two years after the ordeal in the New Hampshire woods, Barney began seeing a psychiatrist to try to deal with his anxiety. Barney and Betty Hill were each hypnotized without the other one present, and the psychiatrist instructed them to forget about their UFO experience once they awoke from their hypnotic states. Although Betty seemed to remember more of the details under hypnosis than Barney (who evidently kept his eyes closed out of fright during most of his experience) did, their accounts of the UFO incident were very similar.

The Hills' psychiatrist, Benjamin Simon, never believed that the Hills had been abducted by aliens, although he thought that they truly believed they had been. He told them their recollections of alien abduction were a fantasy inspired by Betty Hill's vivid nightmares—a contamination-by-dreams hypothesis. Neither of the Hills accepted Simon's di-

agnosis, but they agreed that their therapy had been success-
ful since their stress and anxiety were gone. Other skeptics
note that Betty's description of the aliens matched an alien
that had appeared on the television show *The Outer Limits*
just two weeks before their hypnosis sessions began.

The Pascagoula Case

After the Hills, few abductions were reported until the early
1970s, when several abductions were reported around the
same time. Probably the second-most famous abduction
case after the Hill abduction is the Pascagoula case. On October 11, 1973, Charles Hickson and Calvin Parker were
fishing on the Pascagoula River in Mississippi when, they al-
lege, a UFO appeared behind them. The men described the
spaceship as a domed, football-shaped object about thirty
feet long, ten feet high, with two windows and two blue
lights. According to Hickson and Parker, a door opened and
three aliens came floating out toward them. Hickson
thought the beings looked like gray robots with no necks
and claws for arms. Their mouths were like slits, they had
pointed noses, small eyes, and elephant-like skin. Hickson
said he felt a stinging sensation when two of the aliens came
over and grabbed his arms, and then he became paralyzed.
He saw that Parker had fainted and was being supported by
the third alien. The aliens then guided the two men into the
spaceship. Hickson said he was kept suspended in midair
while a small device, which he called an "eye," passed
around his body, apparently examining him or taking
X rays. Shortly thereafter, the two men were escorted back to
the dock where they had been fishing and the aliens and
their ship disappeared.

After the spaceship left, the two men tried to calm down
by discussing their experience. Hickson opened a bottle of
whiskey while they talked. Parker told Hickson that he had

passed in and out of consciousness during his ordeal, but he remembered being taken into the ship and seeing the bright interior of the spacecraft. When he came to, he was standing outside, but he was unable to move.

The two men called the nearby Keesler Air Force Base in Biloxi, but they were told to call the local sheriff because the Air Force did not take UFO reports. Hickson and Parker then drove to the Jackson County sheriff's office, where they were given a breathalyzer test and were interviewed for two hours. The men did not change their story, even when they were put alone into a room and were secretly tape-recorded. The sheriff thought that, if they were lying, they would talk about how they were fooling the sheriff once they were left alone. Instead, the two men talked about what had happened to them and then knelt in prayer.

By the next day the story of the abduction had made national news. Two scientists flew in to talk with Hickson and Parker. James A. Harder was an engineering professor and a consultant to the Aerial Phenomena Research Organization (APRO) in Tucson, Arizona. J. Allen Hynek was an astronomer and the lead researcher in charge of the U.S. Air Force's Project Blue Book. Harder attempted to hypnotize Hickson (Parker refused to talk about his experience any more) to uncover more memories, but he ended the session early because Hickson appeared too frightened and shaken to continue.

Most investigators who interviewed Hickson and Parker believed that the two men believed they saw a UFO; however, ufologists noted that their description of the aliens did not resemble any other alien reports. After the excitement died down, Parker moved to his home 130 miles north of Pascagoula, where he suffered a nervous breakdown. Hickson eventually took a lie-detector test, which showed that he believed what he was telling investigators to be true.

Pat Roach

A few days after Hickson and Parker reported their abduction by aliens, Pat Roach, a single mother in Lehi, Utah, awoke during the night thinking there had been a prowler in the house. Her children were crying, and the cat was acting crazy. She called the police, gathered up her children, and spent the rest of the night at a friend's house. The next day her seven-year-old daughter, Dottie, reassured her mother: "It wasn't a prowler, Mama, it was a spaceman."[3]

Roach did not undergo hypnosis to explore her memories of that October night until two years later. Under hypnosis, she remembered two figures—about four feet tall and very thin with slanted eyes and claws for hands—standing over her inside her house. This was the first time that an abductee claimed that the aliens had entered a home to perform the abduction. Roach claimed that she and three of her children were floated on a bright light into a room in a spaceship where they were questioned about feelings and emotions. Roach said, "They wanted to know how our minds work . . . to give them certain information that they don't have yet. . . . How we think. How we feel. Our emotions."[4] Under hypnosis, Dottie said much the same thing. An alien "five feet five inches tall, bald on top of his head with a fringe on the sides, dressed in black, wearing horn-rimmed glasses and a rubber glove . . . asked 'what I love, what I hate. What animals I like. They asked me about my family. They manipulated me.'"[5] Dottie also said she saw her neighbors standing in line waiting for their examination.

Many more accounts of contact and abductions were reported in October and November 1973 with details that were similar to those of Hickson and Parker in Pascagoula and Roach in Utah—gray aliens with wrinkled elephant skin and clawlike hands. However, one of the more widely publicized cases happened two years later, in November

1975, near Heber, Arizona, in which six men claimed they witnessed aliens abducting their friend.

The Travis Walton Abduction

Travis Walton, a tree cutter, was heading home with six other cutters in a pickup truck at the end of a long workday. The workers saw a light glowing through the trees ahead and urged the driver, Mike Rogers, to head toward it. Driving along a narrow track through the woods, they came to a clearing where a glowing disk-shaped object was hovering about fifteen feet above the trees. Walton got out of the truck and walked toward the ship. "I was afraid it would fly away and I would miss the chance of a lifetime to satisfy my curiosity about it," he wrote later. As Walton prepared to return to the truck, the other six men saw a bluish green beam of light come out of the ship and strike Walton. The beam lifted Walton a foot off the ground, his arms and legs outstretched, before blasting him back about ten feet and leaving him sprawled on the ground. Walton said of the experience, "I saw and heard nothing. All I felt was a numbing force of a blow that felt like a high-voltage electrocution."[6]

Walton's coworkers yelled at Rogers to leave, and Rogers quickly backed up and turned around. He drove so fast down the dirt track to get out of the woods that when he swerved to miss a tree, the truck skidded into a pile of dirt and stopped. Shaken and scared, the men got out of the truck and saw a sky filled with nothing but stars. Then they started talking about what they should do next; eventually, they decided to return to look for Walton. As Rogers got back in the truck, he saw a whoosh of white light in the sky streaking away from them. He thought it was probably the spaceship leaving.

When the men finally returned to the spot where Walton had left the truck, they could find no sign of him. After searching with flashlights for about twenty minutes, the men decided they needed to notify the police. They drove to a shopping center and called the sheriff's office, telling the dispatcher that Walton was missing and perhaps dead. A search party, organized that evening, failed to find any sign of Walton, or any sign that either he or a UFO had been present in the clearing just a few hours earlier. The search continued the next morning with still no luck in finding Walton.

The sheriff was understandably suspicious about the story being told by Rogers and the other workers. He believed that they had killed him—either accidentally or intentionally—and were covering up his death with a story about a UFO. Walton's coworkers were interviewed extensively by the sheriff, and later by ufologists, and they were given polygraph tests. Five of the men passed the polygraph test; the results from the sixth worker, Allen Dalis, who was not a good friend of Walton, were inconclusive. Cy Gilson, who administered the lie detector tests, wrote in his conclusions,

> These polygraph examinations prove that these five men did see some object that they believe to be a UFO, and that Travis Walton was not injured or murdered by any of these men [on the day of the incident]. If an actual UFO did not exist and the UFO is a man-made hoax, five of these men had no prior knowledge of a hoax. No such determination can be made of the sixth man whose test results were inconclusive.[7]

Five days later Grant Neff, Walton's brother-in-law and one of the men who was with Walton when he disappeared, received a phone call around midnight. It was Walton, saying he was at a phone booth at a gas station in Heber, about thirty miles away, and that he was hurt and needed help. Neff picked up Walton's brother Duane and drove to Heber. There they found Walton slumped over a phone and seemingly in shock. Walton was astounded to learn that he had been missing for five days; he thought it had only been a few hours since he had been struck by the light beam.

The next day Walton was examined by two doctors, they found him to be in good health with no bruises or signs of trauma, which might be expected if a man had been picked up and thrown onto the ground. Two days later, Walton met with Harder from APRO, who hypnotically regressed Walton to learn what had happened to him during the five days he was missing. Walton remembered waking up in what he thought was a hospital room. Slowly, he noticed three figures standing around him. He described them as

> short, shorter than five feet, and they had very large, bald heads, no hair. Their heads were domed, very large. They looked like fetuses. They had no eyebrows, no eyelashes. They had very large eyes—enormous eyes—almost all brown, without much white in them. The creepiest thing about them were those eyes. Oh, man, those eyes, they just stared through me. Their mouths and ears and noses seemed real small, maybe just because their eyes were so huge.[8]

When the beings left, Walton ran out of the room and into a curving hallway. He entered a round, domed room, sat down in the room's only chair, and noticed that the room's light had faded and he could see the stars outside through the walls. He fiddled with a button on the arm of the chair and the stars appeared to move. Then a human-looking being with a clear helmet on his head entered the room. The stranger took Walton's arm and led him out. They walked to what appeared to be a hangar deck with another three or four spaceships like the one he saw in the woods. Walton and his guide then left and went into another room where three more humanlike aliens were waiting. They gestured to him to get up on the examining table; when he did, they put a mask over his face and he lost consciousness again.

The next thing Walton remembered was lying on the

highway in Heber, ten miles from where he had seen the UFO. Of the five days Walton was gone, this was all he said he could remember. While still under hypnosis, Walton told Harder that he would die if he remembered anymore of what happened to him while he was missing. Against Harder's advice, Walton took a polygraph test. Harder believed that Walton was still feeling anxiety from the abduction, and since the test measures stress, he did not want Walton to take it. The polygraph test's questions were given by a skeptic who openly doubted Walton's story during the administration of the test. The test giver, John McCarthy, believed Walton failed the test; APRO's advisers, however, felt the test results were inconclusive due to Walton's anxiety levels so soon after his reappearance. APRO withheld both the fact that Walton took a polygraph test and the results of that test from the public and the sheriff. Eventually, however, Phil Klass, a prominent UFO skeptic, discovered that McCarthy still had Walton's polygraph test and released the results, leading many ufologists and the public to believe Walton's abduction was a hoax.

The Controversy

Many books were published during the 1980s and the 1990s by people who either claimed they were abducted by aliens or by ufologists who said hypnosis sessions uncovered accounts of alien abductions in their patients. And despite having no contact with each other, or any familiarity with books on the subject, the accounts of the abductions were strikingly similar to each other and to the story told by the Hills, Roach, Hickson and Parker, and Walton. In addition, many abductees have scars on their bodies that they claim are "scoop marks" where aliens removed some flesh for further study and research. Some also assert that the aliens have implanted devices into their bodies to track them. The implants mysteriously appeared in the abductees' bodies one day and, for many, just as mysteriously disappeared. Many implants have been surgically removed by doctors; ufologists who have examined the implants claim they are of alien origin, whereas skeptics assert the implants are made of materials common on Earth. Ufologists maintain that the abductees were all solid, reliable citizens who had no reason to lie; these researchers assert that because so many people who have nothing to gain are telling the same story about alien abductions, and since there is no other explanation for the stories, the phenomena of alien abduction must be true.

Skeptics have many reasons to doubt the claims of alien abduction. First of all, they point out there is no physical proof of an abduction. They assert that simply because an alleged abductee is a good citizen does not mean that his or her testimony can be trusted. The skeptics note that many so-called abductees end up telling their stories on television, which, for some people, is a powerful incentive to lie. Many doubters believe that "abductees" are either stressed, suffering from a mental illness, prone to fantasies, or have false memories implanted through hypnosis by incompetent or unethical therapists. They suggest that shared experiences such as alien abduction may just be a delusion inspired and encouraged by a culture that believes in such fantastical beliefs as God, Satan, angels, near-death experiences, psychic phenomena, and the Loch Ness monster. In addition, having a scar of unknown origin is not proof of an alien abduction, the skeptics reason. Many people have scars on their body that they can no longer remember getting. As for the implants, the skeptics argue that after doctors have removed them, scientists have found the implants to be nothing out of the ordinary.

The issues involved in alien abductions are typical of all

other aspects concerning UFOs and aliens. There is no physical proof, or at least no evidence that skeptics are willing to accept as proof that people have been abducted by aliens. Believers of alien abductions maintain that the fact that thousands of people around the world report similar experiences, all without meeting or discussing the details with each other, is proof that the events are real. The authors in the following chapters present evidence both supporting and debunking the phenomenon of alien abduction.

Notes

1. Quoted in David M. Jacobs, ed., *UFOs and Abductions: Challenging the Borders of Knowledge.* Lawrence: University Press of Kansas, 2000, p. 196.

2. Quoted in Jerome Clark, *The UFO Book: Encyclopedia of the Extraterrestrial.* Detroit, MI: Visible Ink Press, 1998, pp. 274, 276.

3. Quoted in Robert E. Bartholomew and George S. Howard, *UFOs and Alien Contact: Two Centuries of Mystery.* Amherst, NY: Prometheus, 1998, p. 352.

4. Quoted in Bartholomew and Howard, *UFOs and Alien Contact,* p. 352.

5. Quoted in Bartholomew and Howard, *UFOs and Alien Contact,* p. 352.

6. Quoted in Kevin D. Randle, *The Randle Report: UFOs in the Nineties.* New York: M. Evans, 1997, pp. 12, 13.

7. Quoted in Clark, *The UFO Book,* p. 633.

8. Quoted in Clark, *The UFO Book,* p. 646.

Chapter 1

Fact or Fiction?

The Evidence
in Support of
Alien Abductions

The Principal Features of Alien Abductions

John E. Mack

People who have been abducted by aliens have similar experiences. Therapists can determine how likely a claim of abduction is by comparing the experience with other known cases of alien abduction. If there are no significant differences, chances are the person has been abducted by aliens. Abductees are usually alone (but not always) when the aliens appear. They are unable to resist the aliens, who transport them in a beam of light to their spaceship. Once inside the spaceship, many abductees are forced to undergo a medical exam by the aliens who either insert or remove an implant into the abductee's body. Sometimes the abductees are forced to undergo an intrusive sexual procedure. John E. Mack is a professor of psychiatry at Harvard Medical School. He is the founding director of Program for Extraordinary Experience Research (PEER) which studies alien abductions. He has written several books about aliens and alien abduction, including *Abduction, Human Encounters with Aliens,* and *Passport to the Cosmos: Human Transformation and Alien Encounters.*

Unlike many syndromes in medicine or psychiatry, it is difficult to enumerate the basic features of the abduction phenomenon in a straightforward, linear fashion. There are several reasons for this. For example, the experiences seem to change over time for particular abductees, depending on the approach that the facilitator uses and the changes of consciousness that take place for a particular experiencer. Furthermore, the shape or evolution of the experience, and even what may be considered the basic elements of the phenomenon itself, will be affected by the clinical background or consciousness of the facilitator and/or by what he or she can accept or tolerate within his or her own psyche or worldview. My own list of the important features of the phenomenon has expanded as I have explored it more deeply. While most investigators might agree on the first item on my list, there might be less concurrence in regard to the five that follow. That points to one of the more frustrating aspects of this kind of research—the fact that researchers have attained only a limited degree of consensus regarding the contours, scope, and meanings associated with this strange phenomenon.

Since this viewpoint is concerned with possible explanations of the abduction phenomenon, it seems to me worthwhile to set forth its complex dimensions in sufficient detail (even then, many important elements will have to be left out because of space limitations) to provide a caution to anyone who might wish to offer a theory, for an explanation to be taken seriously must account for *all* of the basic elements. There is a tendency in this field for critics to pick out one or two elements from the cluster of features that constitute the abduction phenomenon and then make up a theory based on only those few elements. Because the phenomenon often occurs at night and the experiencer may not be able to move, for example, sleep paralysis has been offered as an explanation,[1] even though some abductees insist they are wide awake and abductions can occur in the course of daytime waking life. Because UFOs seem to contain rounded enclosures, the possibility that we are dealing with womb or pregnancy fantasies has been put forth.[2] Or because sudden shifts of consciousness occur during abductions and these can be brought about by temporal lobe stimulation, some sort of temporal lobe activation might be behind it all. One psychiatrist even suggested at a conference that we might be dealing with a variation on an eating problem, since a client whose case I presented had had a period of anorexia, and eating disorders were this psychiatrist's specialty.

The Abduction Begins

Abduction experiences appear to concentrate in families, sometimes over several generations. They seem curiously "democratic," as no distinction by race, gender, socioeconomic status, or age has been discovered. Although experiencers may ask to be seen in order to explore a particularly well-remembered event, it may turn out that they have had many such experiences during their lifetime. Memory behaves oddly in relation to abductions, which makes poll-taking a hazardous adventure, for what is "forgotten" one day may be remembered the next. Something more than ordinary repression seems to be at work here, for understandable psychological motives for remembering or forgetting can be difficult to identify.

Characteristically, abductees are in their bedroom or some other room at night, driving a car, or, in the case of children, playing outside when the experience begins. They may or may not see a UFO close by. They then may sense a "presence," or that "they" (unidentified beings) are nearby. They may hear an audible humming sound or, more frequently, see an intense, bright light that fills the room, or experience some other sort of vibratory or "electrical" energy.[3] One or more small beings may be seen close by, who, "real" or not, possess features that have become firmly embedded in popular culture and contemporary lore. They are characteristically three to four feet tall, with disproportionately large, bald heads that protrude in the back, grayish tan facial skin that is variously wrinkled, huge oval pupil-less black eyes, rudimentary noses with nostril holes, small slitlike mouths, thin bodies, spindly legs and arms, hands with three or four long fingers, and a one-piece tuniclike garment for clothing. These so-called gray beings move, float, or glide about easily, their movements sometimes being described as robotic. Their communication is always telepathic or mind to mind. In addition, other reptilian, luminous, insectlike, or even more human-appearing beings have also been identified inside or outside of what appear to be spacecraft.

Experiencing great fear—at least until the reality is confronted or the beings do something to calm them (touching with a hand or rod, reassuring the experiencer that he or she will be all right)—the abductees find themselves unable to move. In this paralyzed state the experiencers are "floated"— the word they virtually always use—out of the room, down a hall, and right through the window, door, or ceiling of the house, usually accompanied by the beings, with a beam of light that emanates from some outside source providing the energy that moves them. They may see their house or neighborhood recede below them as they are moved up and into a waiting spacecraft—either a small podlike vessel that takes them to the "mother ship" or directly into a large craft. Cu-

riously, the experiencers do not feel cold as they travel upward, and they may sense that this is because they are pro-
tected by some sort of tube or tunnel of light or other form
of energy that surrounds them. Witnesses to this event are
rare,[4] but the experiences are so intensely physical that abductees feel quite certain that some, though not all, of the
time their physical form, as opposed to their astral or other
forms of the subtle body, are taken.

Intrusive Medical/Surgical Procedures

Once inside the craft, the experiencer may see more beings
moving about purposefully in cool rooms with curved walls
that may contain a musty or other unpleasant smell.
Around the walls, which have no apparent corners, complex
computer-like equipment may be seen, and various sorts of
recessed or mobile lighting are visible. The experiencer, who
has usually had most, if not all, of his or her clothes taken
along the way, is usually next placed on a table, although
abductees may be shown about the ship and often see other
abductees like themselves there. The activities seem to be
under the direction of a leader figure, who usually is described as a little taller than the other alien "drones."

On the table the abductee is stared at, sometimes close
up, by one or more of the beings with their large black eyes
and is subjected to a variety of medical/surgical-like procedures with instruments with which we are not generally familiar. These include probing of various orifices of the body
through the eyes, nose, ears, navel, and rectum. The abductees may feel or be told that they are being checked up
on, their health monitored or even in some way healed.
Sometimes they experience an "implant" has been inserted
in their bodies, a kind of tag, which allows the aliens, they
believe, to follow or find them in the future. Various tiny
objects, which the abductees have identified as implants,

have been removed from under the skin. The results of the analysis of these objects have been controversial, with some researchers[5] failing to find any convincing evidence that they are of extraterrestrial or other unusual origin, while others[6] are convinced that they are truly unusual.

Budd Hopkins,[7] David M. Jacobs,[8] and other investigators (including myself) have documented that some sort of complex, reproductive-like process or "project" appears to be a central feature of the UFO abduction phenomenon, beginning sometimes with sperm being taken from men by forced ejaculation and eggs from women via the vagina. After a sequence of abduction experiences, strange fetuses that become babies and then small children seem to be created. These are seen in the ships by the abductees on subsequent abductions, and they are encouraged to nourish these odd hybrid creatures, who do appear as a kind of cross between human and alien beings. One of the most convincing aspects of the phenomenon is the intense maternal distress of women who recall with certainty that they have been presented with their own hybrid offspring but have no say about when they will be able to see these creatures again. After the procedures are completed, the abductee is returned to, or close to, the place from which he or she was taken. Odd, even humorous, mistakes seem to occur—the person being returned, for example, to the bed the wrong way around or with clothes on backward, or a child may be tucked too tightly into its bed.

Energetic Elements

Even a brief acquaintance with the UFO/abduction field will show that there are extraordinary energies involved.[9] These range from the propulsion system of UFOs themselves to the experience of cellular change that abductees feel they have undergone during their experiences. Some sort of intense, high-frequency vibrations seem to be present in the room when the alien beings arrive. Brilliant light emanates from the craft and may flood the area where the abduction begins. The abductees report being moved mysteriously on a beam of light or by some other energy or force out of their rooms or cars and into the craft. Strange, rapid healing processes have been observed,[10] which seem to be brought about by some sort of energy that the experiencers feel certain of but cannot explain.

When they are taken or floated through the wall, ceiling, or window of their homes or through the door of a car, the abductees feel as if an intense energy is separating every cell, or even every molecule, of their bodies. So powerful is this feeling that experiencers often find it remarkable that they "come back together" whole on the other side of the wall. After their experiences, abductees characteristically feel that powerful residual energies are left in their bodies, as if stored in the cells themselves. Interestingly, in an EEG study Don and Moura showed that abductees reveal a hyperarousal state comparable only to those of advanced meditators or yogis when they are encouraged to relive their experiences imaginatively.[11] Nothing else in my clinical experience has ever quite reached the dramatic intensity of the release of these energies during the relaxation sessions in which the abduction experiences are relived. The abductees speak of powerful vibratory sensations in their arms, legs, and other parts of their bodies. It feels to them as if every cell in their bodies is vibrating, and their bodies may literally shake or "vibrate" on the couch as the experience is recalled or relived. Bloodcurdling screams or loud sobbing may help to relieve the tension they feel.[12]

Knowledge: Protecting the Earth

Many abductees feel that through the probing or by contact with the large black eyes that the beings are studying or "downloading" information from their minds and brains. At the same time the experiencers frequently feel that knowledge has been *given* to them through the eyes, telepathically, in scenes and symbols shown to them on the ships on television-like monitors, or even through "libraries" that may appear to hold books or to be contained in balls of light. From this information the abductees may feel that they have acquired understanding of subjects they have not otherwise studied, or have gained special insights or psychic abilities. Credo Mutwa, a renowned Zulu shaman, for example, feels certain that his abilities as an artist and his knowledge of science and technology came to him from the Mantindane, the Zulu word he uses for beings that seem quite like the grays described in Western reports.[13]

Often the information that abductees take in concerns the earth, its jeopardy, and human responsibility for the future of the planet's life. Sometimes the "lessons" are conveyed through apocalyptic images of destruction of the earth's life or even of the earth itself. These may be juxtaposed with other scenes of transcendent beauty, which may leave the experiencers emotionally shaken. In one abduction experience Jim Sparks, formerly a real estate developer, was shown scene after scene of magnificent earth landscapes, followed by images of the same areas now devastated by pollution and erosion. Several of the children at the Ariel School in Zimbabwe, who witnessed the landing of several UFOs in September 1994, reported that the beings conveyed through their eyes that we were not taking "proper care" of the planet.[14]

The impact of this information about the state of the planet may affect abductees profoundly. They may feel a visceral identification with the earth itself, which becomes for them a kind of living organism, and may feel a sense of despair. Some experiencers will devote their lives to protecting the earth and become active, directly or indirectly, in ecologically related efforts. Abduction researchers and abductees themselves disagree about the possible motives behind such experiences. Some are convinced these entities love the planet and wish to protect it, while others cynically conclude that the beings are trying to protect the planet for their own agendas, or even that they are simply testing our reactions as part of a human study program. It often seems that, in this and other instances, the attribution of motive or intention to the beings, since we cannot really know what they are trying to do, reflects more the psyche and outlook of the witness than anything else.[15]

Symbols and Shamans

Abduction researchers have frequently observed that the alien beings, especially the typical grays, sometimes appear initially to the experiencers as familiar animals. Owls, eagles, raccoons, and deer are a few of the animal forms in which the beings have been initially perceived. Less well appreciated is the fact that these animal representations are not simply forms of disguise but may have symbolic meaning or may have some connection with the psyche of the experiencer. Brazilian shaman Bernardo Peixoto told me that the Ikuyas (the word that his tribe uses for entities that seem to resemble our gray beings) will represent themselves to abduction experiencers in a form that connects with the animal spirit or spirits associated with a particular individual.[16]. . .

The Search for Alternative Explanations

The descriptions provided here give only a sketchy summary of some of the principal features of the abduction phenomenon. Researchers do differ with regard to some of the details, or what should be emphasized, and certainly do not agree on the possible meanings and implications of the phenomenon, which lie beyond the scope of this viewpoint. But even this brief overview should suggest that no psychiatric condition or obvious other psychophysiological or sociocultural explanation can account for all, or even most, of the vast range of elements that constitute the phenomenon, only a fraction of which have been described here.

It is my view that we would not even search so hard for alternative, "conventional" (conventional in terms of our culture's definitions of reality) explanations were it not for the fact that the abduction phenomenon as reported so violates the prevailing worldview of scientific materialism or anthropocentric humanism. Indeed, none of the scores of explanations proposed, from sleep paralysis to media contamination to mass delusion, accounts, even potentially, for more than a small fraction of the many elements that make up the full picture. The search for alternative explanations will, and perhaps must, continue if for no other reason than that this is part of the process by which inadequate ontologies weaken and lose their hold on the human mind.

Perhaps now it will not be long before we, as a society, may let go of resistance and fear of the unknown, and appreciate that the abduction phenomenon, near-death experiences, the experiments of parapsychology, and other well-documented anomalies that challenge the Western worldview are forcing us to change our thinking about who we are and the nature of the cosmos in which we exist. We may then be able to accept the UFO/abduction phenomenon for what it seems to be, namely, the penetration into our minds and worlds of physical objects and strange beings brought into our reality by a mysterious intelligence whose purposes or intention we can only surmise. Such acceptance might allow us to encounter and explore the phenomenon in its own right, including its more disturbing aspects, and get on with the exciting project of learning more deeply about its nature and meaning for our current lives and future possibilities.

Notes

1. Robert A. Baker and Joe Nickell, *Missing Pieces* (Buffalo, N.Y.: Prometheus Books, 1992).

2. Alvin H. Lawson, "Perinatal Imagery in UFO Abduction Reports," *Journal of Psychohistory* 122 (1984): 211–39.

3. John E. Mack, *Abduction*, revised paperback edition (New York: Ballantine, 1995), chap. 6.

4. Budd Hopkins, *Witnessed: The True Story of the Brooklyn Bridge UFO Abductions* (New York: Pocket Books, 1996).

5. David E. Pritchard, "Physical Evidence and Abductions," in *Alien Discussions: Proceedings of the Alien Abduction Study Conference Held at MIT*, ed. Andrea Pritchard, David E. Pritchard, Pam Kasey, and Claudia Yapp (Cambridge, Mass.: North Cambridge Press, 1994), pp. 279–95.

6. Roger K. Leir, *The Aliens and the Scalpel: Scientific Proof of Extraterrestrial Implants in Humans* (Columbus, N.C.: Granite Publishing, 1998).

7. Budd Hopkins, *Missing Time: A Documented Study of UFO Abductions* (New York: Marek, 1981).

8. David M. Jacobs, *The Threat: The Secret Alien Agenda* (New York: Simon and Schuster, 1998).

9. Jacques Vallee, *Confrontations: A Scientist's Search for Alien Contact* (New York: Ballantine, 1990); Paul Hill, *Unconventional Flying Objects: A Scientific Analysis* (Charlottesville, Va.: Hampden Roads, 1995).

10. Preston Dennett, *UFO Healings* (Mill Spring, N.C.: Wild Flower Press, 1996).

11. Norman Don and Gilda Moura, "Topographic Brain Mapping of UFO Experiencers," *Journal of Scientific Exploration* 11 (1997): 435–53.

12. For further discussion of the light and energy aspects of the abduction phenomenon, see John Mack, *Passport to the Cosmos* (New York: Crown, 1999), chap. 4.

13. Stephen Larsen, ed., *Songs of the Stars: The Lore of a Zulu Shaman (Vusamazulu Credo Mutwa)*, with a foreword by Luisah Teish

(Barrytown, N.Y.: Barrytown, 1996).

14. Dominique Callimanopulos, "Exploring African and Other Abductions," *Centerpiece*, spring–summer 1995, pp. 10–11.

15. Further discussion of this aspect of the abduction phenomenon can be found in Mack, *Passport to the Cosmos*, chap. 5.

16. Personal communication, 10 May 1998.

Alien Abductions Occur Worldwide

Scott Corrales

While reports of alien abductions are prevalent in the United States, they occur throughout the world. A considerable number of alien abductions have been reported in Puerto Rico, Mexico, and Spain. The Hispanic abductees report experiences that are similar to those in English-speaking countries, but their accounts are met with greater skepticism. This lack of willingness to accept the veracity of alien abductions has kept many abductees from telling their stories and therapists from helping abductees. Scott Corrales is the editor of *Inexplicata: The Journal of Hispanic Ufology* and a frequent contributor to *Fate* magazine.

While instances of alleged abduction by UFO aliens are rife in North America, they are considerably less prevalent in the Spanish/Portuguese-speaking regions of the world.

This is all the more curious considering that one of the earliest cases, and the one most readily memorable, is without
question the Antonio Villas-Boas abduction (Brazil, 1952).
Its graphic retelling of the victim's overpowering by hel-
meted aliens, the oft-mentioned sexual interlude with a
space "siren" and the severe physiological aftereffects suffered by Villas-Boas rocked the nascent discipline of ufology
to the core. But that was in days long gone by, when UFO
abductions involved the physical interference with a single
or many humans in a deserted location, usually a rural
highway, a desert, or a forest—way before the ubiquitous
"Greys" were transporting helpless experiencers through
their bedroom walls, inducing pregnancies, and involving
them in apparent genetic studies.

Comparative analysts such as T.E. Bullard have pointed
out that the abduction phenomenon is largely an American
one, with one of every two cases coming out of the U.S. and
Canada—half of all abduction experiences are "made in the
U.S.A." This gives us another half distributed around the
rest of the planet, and the Spanish-speaking regions of the
world certainly have their fair share.

Unfortunately, the importance of abduction research
overshadowed conventional encounters with nonhuman
entities: the so-called traditional cases, which usually involved a nocturnal encounter by a roadside, the accidental
encounter with a landed saucer and its occupants, and other
forms of human/nonhuman contact that did not fit into the
clearly defined parameters of the abduction phenomenon.

It is perhaps of interest to investigators that this traditional type of case continues to occur, often far beyond our
borders. What is the *modus operandi* of the abductors in
these locations? Are there any Greys, Nordics, or other non-
humans involved? Is hypnosis a tool of choice, as it is in
North America? We shall examine a number of these cases.

An Abduction Through Meditation?

Puerto Rico, notorious for its intense UFO activity and the depredations of the now-legendary *chupacabras*, boasts a considerable number of UFO abduction cases. One of these cases stands out among the others due to the possibility that the experiencer's efforts at meditation "opened up" a path for abducting Greys to enter her life.

Delia V, a housewife with two children, had no idea that her interest in yoga would turn her into an abductee when she and a friend visited a yoga temple in October 1991 to practice meditative techniques. At 7:30 P.M., Delia decided to withdraw from the meditation circle and go to bed early. Once in bed, she felt a hand covering her face. She was unable to see her assailant due to the darkness in the bedroom. It was then that she became aware of the fact that she was flying in mid-air toward a given point in space: buildings, streets, and automobiles remained far below Delia as she drifted upward. Far from feeling elated at the sight, she was paralyzed by fear.

The next thing she remembers is being back in bed at the yoga temple at five o'clock in the morning, feeling sick to her stomach and racked by excruciating pain. Stumbling out of her room, she told the meditation instructor what had happened, and he advised her to simply return to sleep, which she did. Reawakening at noon, not only did she feel physically better, her entire outlook on life had been changed, by her own admission.

During the following months, some physical changes had also come about as a consequence of that unusual night: Her menstrual cycle now ran every 50 days or so, and her stomach became slightly enlarged.

A subsequent event revealed the UFO connection to her experiences: Shortly after seeing a brilliant craft in the sky, she found herself standing in a metallic chamber occupied by a dozen or so very small, nonhuman beings clad in gray. Delia remembers lying on a bed, screaming and crying, telling one of the bizarre figures that she could not give normal birth to the child she was carrying because her other children had been born by Caesarean section. "When I woke up," Delia says, "I saw one of the extraterrestrials with a child in his arms. When I saw this child something deep inside me told me he was my child, but I also remember being afraid. I remember telling one of the extraterrestrials that I considered this child strange, because he was half-human and half-extraterrestrial." Delia was then given the child to hold, and was told by the creatures that it could not live among humans because it could not eat human food.

Delia's case echoes the hundreds of abduction experiences collected by U.S. investigators. It has been observed that Puerto Rican abduction cases have a stronger environmental content to them than those on the mainland. Experiencers are imparted messages of ecological importance and cases involving hybridization are few. The *modus operandi* of the abductors remains slightly behind the times—the controversial Amaury Rivera case (1988) involved interference with the experiencer's vehicle. Other cases in which humans in lonely areas or alone at a late hour have been victims of abductions are also on file.

Assaulted by Aliens

Books and magazine articles dealing with the very real perils, both mental and physical, suffered by experiencers of the UFO phenomenon are commonplace today. Distinguished ufologists such as David Jacobs openly state that the involvement of nonhuman intelligences in human events may not be so sanguine as many had firmly believed in earlier decades—that UFO occupants were here to help us take the next evolutionary step or eventually render assistance in solving humanity's most pressing problems. The eerie experience of a hapless Mexican ceramics technician should have given researchers early warning when it occurred more than twenty years ago.

In 1972, researchers Jorge Reichert and Salvador Freixedo looked into the experiences of Heriberto Garza, who allegedly had repeated encounters with otherworldly entities. Garza, a tall slender man who lived in the city of Puebla with his only son, had been unwilling to go public with his paranormal experiences for fear of being ostracized by the conservative residents of his community.

His experience began as he was getting ready to go to bed one night. After turning off the light and getting between the sheets, he heard an unusual noise in the living room. Fearing that a break-in was in progress, he promptly went to investigate and was surprised to find a tall man with distinguished, almost feminine facial features. Taken aback, Garza demanded to know how this figure had entered his apartment. The entity told him in perfect Spanish that it could obviate physical obstacles and go where it pleased— but the reason for its visit was to grant Heriberto Garza "an experience that many would wish to have." His involvement with creatures from an improbable world known as Auko was about to begin.

Garza claimed to have subsequently been taken aboard a spacecraft, where he met other beings similar in appearance to his original contact. One alien took his left hand and drew blood from his ring finger before returning him to his apartment, a return trip which he did not remember. He suddenly found himself sitting on an easy chair back home, with the door to the outside hallway open.

Strange phenomena began to occur soon after this experience. One morning, while shaving in front of the bathroom mirror, Garza saw his reflection vanish, only to reappear as he heard alien voices ringing in his ears, bearing a message that he was unable to understand. He would soon be subjected to intense telepathic communication with his nonhuman "friends," the consequences of which led him to seek psychiatric advice.

During a follow-up visit with researcher Ian Norris, Reichert was perplexed by the change in Heriberto Garza's demeanor. The once-articulate man spoke sluggishly and did not appear to be himself. At one point, Garza said: "I want to show you what is happening to me" and proceeded to unbutton his shirt. The researchers were astounded to see a number of nipples growing randomly across Garza's abdomen, some of them small, others larger and with abundant hair. Reichert and Freixedo concluded that something had been injected into Garza that tampered with his DNA. Detailed study of the case became impossible when the experiencer "disappeared." Visitors to the humble apartment building in Puebla were angrily turned away by Garza's son, whose father appears to have become an early casualty of tampering by uncaring nonhuman forces. . . .

Saucers in Spain

Spain's first recorded UFO abduction was that of Próspera Muñoz in 1947 on the outskirts of Jumilla, a town in the southern province of Murcia, well known as a wine-producing region. While on a farm belonging to one of her uncles, Muñoz and her sister witnessed the presence of a "circular automobile" from which descended two diminutive, large-headed beings who cautioned the girls that very same night "they would return for one of them."

The little aliens made good on their threat and took Próspera to an enormous disk-shaped craft, where she was examined by the occupants and allegedly had a "micro device inserted into her neck." The Muñoz experience, which was not made known until 30 years later, would simply be the introduction to a number of cases involving contact between humans and supposedly nonhuman entities in the Iberian Peninsula.

Fernando Martínez (an alias given him by researcher Manuel Carballal), an electrician from the city of La Coruña in northwestern Spain, never believed that a weekend of motorcrossing on his freshly overhauled dirt bike would have ended in an abduction experience.

Sometime in late October 1986, Fernando drove his bike out to an abandoned stone quarry near Culleredo. Around 9:00 P.M., he suddenly became aware of a "star moving in the sky." The light became larger and larger until it became the size of a full moon. The astonished electrician noticed that the sphere disgorged a number of smaller, orange-colored triangular craft—one of which initiated a rapid descent toward the abandoned quarry.

Realizing his predicament in a flash, Fernando tried to kick-start his dirt bike in vain, even though it had been running perfectly earlier. The UFO was now a large object, some 30 feet wide, hovering over the surface. In the face of the phenomenon, the electrician got off the dirt bike and sat on the ground, waiting to see what would happen next.

Fernando remembers a powerful beam of light emanating from the orange triangle, and two beings descending along the trail of light. The creatures were small and large-headed. They approached Fernando silently, guiding him toward the base of the hovering triangle. Fernando claims to have not felt any fear at the time. No effort at communication was made by his captors.

The next thing he realized was that he stood in a large chamber in which a third being, identical to the other two, came out to meet him, projecting reassuring telepathic messages. He remembers being placed in a horizontal position and feeling pain in one of his arms.

His next conscious memory was that of lying on the gravel of the quarry in Culleredo. The dirt bike now worked perfectly, and the confused electrician made his way home. Two hours of his life were inexplicably unaccounted for.

Seldom does a UFO investigator get to see an unexplained celestial phenomenon that he or she can classify as a UFO with any degree of certainty. Even rarer are the occasions when an investigator manages to get a terrifying glimpse of alien intruders.

In 1991, researcher Josep Guijarro traveled from his home in Barcelona to the island of Gran Canaria (largest of the Canary archipelago) as part of a continuing investigation into the experiences of Judith, a nurse at one of Gran Canaria's hospitals, who had undergone a number of abduction episodes. Her first experience had occurred the previous summer, when she drove into a dense fog bank in her Renault and was found unconscious at the wheel the following morning by another motorist. Subsequent experiences included a number of disturbing "bedroom visitations" by supposedly alien entities.

Guijarro and Judith worked out a plan by which they would try to catch one of these unknown quantities at work: the ufologist would sleep in a bedroom next to that of the experiencer and would try to document "the source of her phobias."

"That night," Guijarro writes in his book *Infiltrados* (Sangrila, 1992), "Judith and I spoke until well into the night, when suddenly her pet dog stood to attention and the TV set's volume control began increasing and decreasing of its own accord. We exchanged a knowing look. When everything appeared to have calmed down, we began hearing the sound of chanting. I cannot deny that I began to feel scared. With a look of fear still etched on my face, I suggested that we go to straightaway. If the Visitors existed, if they were not a figment of our imaginations, this night had all the makings for catching one."

Ufologist and experiencer vanished into their separate chambers. The former readied his camera and tape recorder, lying down in bed with his eyes firmly glued to the open doorway, expecting something to happen. In the darkness, Guijarro claims having heard all manner of creaking and squealing sounds, which he attributed to the structure of the house. At around 3:00 A.M., the dog began to howl and steps could be heard on the staircase.

"It was then that I saw it with stunning tranquility," Guijarro writes. "The outline of a short creature with a large head had just gone past my bedroom's doorway. My reaction to it was equally surprising—I made no movements whatsoever beyond taking a deep breath and falling asleep."

The following day, the ufologist told Judith about his experiences, realizing that while he may have worked himself into a highly suggestible state, that night he had lived the anguishing experience that affected not only his present subject, but tens of thousands of others worldwide.

Aside from the obvious fact of having "witnessed" what could have been one of the large-headed Greys, Josep Guijarro's account is significant due to the occurrence of high strangeness phenomena bordering on the paranormal: the fluctuations in the television set's volume control, the defensive attitude of the household pet and its subsequent howling, and the unnerving sound of "chanting" which prompted both individuals to retire to their rooms—incidents that should give boosters of the ETH (extraterrestrial hypothesis) food for thought.

While the abductions of humans by superhuman forces of varying descriptions appear to obey the same mechanisms worldwide, there has been little support for abductees in Latin America or Spain. A growing number of medical and scientific figures have emerged as champions for the cause, but abduction experiences, as opposed to UFO cases, are met with a greater skepticism that borders on harshness in the Spanish-speaking countries. During a convention of mental-healthcare professionals held in Spain in 1990, a psychiatrist was asked to give his expert opinion on perfectly normal individuals who insisted on having experienced contact with alien creatures. "They're psychotic," the man declared cuttingly. "Anyone who sees things that don't exist is psychotic."

In a report prepared on the case for alien abductions in Spain, analyzing a dozen cases from 1947 to 1979 in which abduction by aliens was an issue, veteran researcher Vicente Juan Ballester Olmos points out: "This systematic review of abduction reports has disclosed that all cases can be reasonably explained in terms which do not defy present-day knowledge . . . it should be emphasized that the resolution of these cases in terms of hoax, delusion, or psychosis has been proposed by dedicated UFO researchers, not by debunkers or dogmatic skeptics; consequently, it is unrealistic to suggest that the interpretations are biased."

In spite of the appearance of very important books on the subject of abductions written in Spanish, namely Manuel Carballal's *Secuestrados por los Ovnis* (Abducted by UFOs) and Josep Guijarro's *Infiltrados* (The Infiltrators), neither one has had the success of Budd Hopkins' *Missing Time* or any one of Whitley Strieber's works. Few Latin American and Spanish psychiatrists have expressed a willingness to handle patients who claim to have been victims of alien abductions (there are notable exceptions, such as Puerto Rico's Manuel Méndez del Toro and the late Francisco Rovatti in Spain), and there is a reticence on the percipients' part to come forward with their experiences.

Hypnosis Can Reveal the Existence of Alien Abduction

David M. Jacobs

While hypnosis is a valuable tool in uncovering the truth behind alien abductions, it is not infallible. However, an experienced and competent hypnotist can determine whether the subject is telling the truth about an alien abduction or whether the subject is prone to accepting misleading suggestions from the hypnotist. People who have truly experienced an alien abduction will resist all the hypnotist's attempts at misleading them. David M. Jacobs is an associate professor of history at Temple University in Philadelphia. He is the author of several books on unidentified flying objects and alien abductions, including *The UFO Controversy, Secret Life: Firsthand Accounts of UFO Abductions*, and *The Threat*.

I have received thousands of calls and letters from people who have memories of unusual experiences that have been greatly disturbing to them. They have searched for years in vain to discover the origin of these memories. They think that I might be able to help them. Of course, a person's experiencing unusual events does not necessarily mean he or she is an abductee. I have designed a screening process to eliminate those people who are not serious about their quest (they might merely be on a lark), those who are not emotionally prepared to look into their experiences, and those who have not had, in my estimation, experiences suggesting that they are abductees.

First, I purposely put them through a series of tasks. I require them to fill out a questionnaire about the experiences that propelled them to come forward, and about others that they might not have realized could be part of the abduction phenomenon (for example, "Have you ever seen a ghost?"). I ask them to send the completed questionnaire to me and then to call back. I analyze the questionnaire and decide if their experiences are significant enough to warrant further investigation with hypnosis. When I talk with them again, I try to persuade them not to look into what could be a Pandora's Box. I give them a strong and frank warning about the dangers of going forward with hypnosis and uncovering an abduction event: They might become depressed, they might have sleep disturbances, they might feel emotionally isolated, and so forth. In effect, they could easily be trading one set of problems for another. I urge them to talk over their decision with their loved ones and call me back later. I then send them a pamphlet that reiterates my warnings so that they can make as informed a decision as possible.

About 30 percent of the people who contact me decide not to undergo hypnosis at this point. This is the right decision for them no matter what their reasons. If they do decide to go forward with the process, I give them another verbal warning about the potential dangers and, if they are still willing, we make an appointment for a session. By the time they arrive for their first hypnosis regression, I have typically already spent several hours talking to them, and they are aware of the problems that might result from their regressions. They are also aware that what they remember, if anything, may not necessarily be accurate or even true.

The First Session

When they finally arrive at my home, we climb the stairs to my third-floor office and talk for an hour or two before we begin hypnosis. We agree about which event in their lives we want to investigate during this session. It might be, for example, a period of missing time, or an incident in which they awoke and found little men standing around their bed. They then lie down on my day-couch and close their eyes, and I begin a simple relaxation induction that allows them to concentrate and focus. At their first session, they are often puzzled because they are not in some "dreamland" or because they feel quite normal. They find that they can argue with me, get up and go to the bathroom, and be completely in control.

I never know what is going to come out of a hypnosis session. If the subject recalls an abduction event—and there are "false alarms," when it seems that an abduction might have taken place but it did not—I begin a series of cautious questions, usually in a conversational style, that organically spring from what they are saying. Some abductees recount their experiences with detachment, as though they were looking back at the past from a present-day standpoint, others relive their memories as if they were the age at which the event took place. Some are calm about what is happening to them, others are so frightened it becomes difficult for them to continue, although I gently help them through the experience. Some remember the events haltingly, as the memories come in spurts and starts. Others have trouble describing their experiences because the memories rush back in a flood. Nearly all abductees recall their experiences with a combination of astonishment, surprise, and familiarity. When they are finished, they remember what happened to them, and we talk about their account for an hour or so. When the abductee leaves my office about five hours have passed.[1]

Even with all my warnings and the preliminary discussions before the first session, about 25 percent stop at this point—usually they are too frightened to go on. For those who continue with me, I conduct as many hypnosis sessions with them as I can. They desperately want to understand what has happened to them and how it has influenced their lives. I have conducted as many as thirty-three sessions with one individual, although the average for all the 110 abductees with whom I have worked is six. I usually do not go over the same event twice.

My style of questioning is not interrogatory. I engage in a give-and-take with the abductee after I am sure that they cannot and will not be led, even inadvertently. I force them to think carefully about the events. I try to give them perspective and the ability to analyze as they remember. Above all, I try to "normalize" them so they can extricate themselves from the unconscious emotional grip the phenomenon often has had them in throughout their lives. I try to give them the strength to untangle themselves from the abductions' psychological effects so that they can get on with their lives without having to constantly think about their situation. I like to get them to the point where they no longer feel the necessity to seek out a hypnotist to understand what has been happening to them.

Few Are Qualified

Hypnosis is easy. As long as a person wants to be hypnotized, anybody can do it. Asking the right questions in the
right way, at the right time, and interpreting the answers is
where the trouble comes in. The correct dynamic between
hypnotist and abductee depends on the amount of knowledge the hypnotist has acquired about the abduction phenomenon, the experience he or she has with hypnosis, and
the preconceptions the hypnotist brings to the session. In
addition, the hypnotist must help the abductee cope with
the sometimes traumatic memories by intervening thera-
peutically during the session to provide context and reas-
surance. Thus, a competent hypnotist/researcher must have
a professional knowledge of hypnosis, a thorough knowledge of the abduction phenomenon, a familiarity with confabulation and false memories, and skill in therapy. Unfortunately, there are few individuals with those qualifications.

All competent researchers quickly learn that memory is
unreliable. It is not unusual for a person to remember details of a "normal" traumatic event inaccurately. Researchers
have shown that they can make people remember something that never happened. A casual, but calculated, discussion of an event with a person can instill "memories" in
him that have no basis in reality. Through the passage of
time, memory also degrades, events blend into one another,
and fantasy intrudes upon reality. . . .

Abduction Confabulation

Abduction confabulation is a frequent problem, especially
in the first few hypnotic sessions. The initial hypnotic session is always the most difficult because it can be very fright-
ening. Many people erroneously think they will blurt out
intimate details of their personal lives, or be at the mercy of
the "evil" hypnotist. Once the first few sessions are com-

pleted, however, the abductee feels more comfortable with the hypnotist and with hypnosis. As a result, his memories become easier to collect and more accurate as well.

Confabulation typically occurs in three characteristic areas.

1. *Physical Appearance of the Aliens.* The most prevalent area of distortion is the description of the physical appearance of the aliens. Many abductees at first maintain that they can see every part of the aliens' bodies except their faces. Some abductees think that the aliens are purposely distorting or limiting the field of view to help prevent the shock of seeing their faces. The evidence does not support this. Because the abduction phenomenon begins in infancy, most abductees have seen the faces of the aliens many times. Once an abductee becomes accustomed to remembering events and less frightened about what he encounters, he usually sees the aliens' faces clearly.

   Also, at first abductees tend to describe the aliens as much taller than they are, not realizing that they are gazing up at the aliens because they are lying on a table. They also describe the aliens as being different colors and having different features. In fact, the majority of aliens are small, gray, and almost featureless except for their large eyes. During competent hypnotic investigation, the abductees recognize their mistakes and correct themselves without the hypnotist's aid or prompting.

2. *Conversation.* Another prevalent area of confabulation is alien dialogue. Although alien conversation has given us our most important insights into the abduction phenomenon's methods and goals, researchers must be extremely cautious.

   Abductees report that all communication with the aliens is telepathic, as is communication among the aliens. When asked what "telepathic" means, the abductees usually say they receive an impression that they automatically translate into words. We know that an abductee can receive an impression from his own thoughts, translate it into his words, and think that the words are coming from aliens. Naive researchers often accept alien dialogue at face value, not realizing that all or portions of it could be generated from the abductee's mind. Abductees sometimes slip into a "channeling" mode—in which the abductee "hears" messages from his own mind and thinks they are coming from outside sources—and the researcher fails to catch it. Some researchers have based much of their knowledge on suspect dialogue. Only experienced researchers can separate characteristic alien conversational patterns from confabulated dialogue.

3. *Alien Intentions*. The third area of confabulation is interpreting alien intentions and goals. For example, when asked about the purpose of a specific mechanical device during an abduction, most abductees answer "I don't know." Some, however, supply an answer because it seems reasonable: "This machine takes pictures of my muscles, sort of like an X-ray machine." Unless the investigator firmly and reliably establishes that the aliens told this to the abductee—and that the abductee did not invent the dialogue—the correct assumption is that the abductee does not know what the machine is for and is simply filling in.

The investigator must also be extremely careful with abductee accounts of what the aliens are doing. The aliens rarely describe the reasons for specific procedures, but some abductees routinely supply the reasons. Again, naive therapists and investigators tend to take these accounts at face value.

Some researchers reinvestigate the same material repeatedly in different hypnotic sessions, not realizing that if the account contains unrecognized confabulation and distortion, it can enter into normal memory as "fact." Repeated hypnosis on an event tends to confirm the "fact," and it often becomes impossible to tell what is real and what is not. On the other hand, the more sessions on different events an abductee has with a competent investigator, the greater the likelihood that confabulation will be uncovered and the accurate account will be told.

Competent Hypnosis

An experienced and competent hypnotist tests the suggestibility of people who recall abduction accounts. By asking purposefully misleading questions, he can easily tell whether the subject can be led. For example, in the first hypnotic session, I often ask if a subject can see the "flat, broad" chins of the aliens. I ask if a subject can see the corners of the ceiling; I ask if the aliens are fat. The answer to these questions should be "no" according to all the evidence we have obtained. If the answer is "yes," I allow for the suggestibility of the subject when I evaluate the truthfulness and accuracy of the account.

Researcher John Carpenter of Springfield, Missouri, has fashioned this line of questioning into something of a science. He has developed a list of misleading questions—some obvious and some subtle—that are calculated to place wrong images into abductees' minds. In the first hypnotic session, he poses these questions to the new subject, who almost never answers "yes"; most abductees refuse to be led and nearly always answer misleading questions negatively, directly contradicting or correcting the hypnotist.

The first abduction incident that received widespread publicity, the Barney and Betty Hill case, published in magazine and book form in 1966, is an excellent example of the lack of suggestibility among abductees. Using hypnosis, psychiatrist Benjamin Simon tried to trap the Hills in contradictions and to suggest to them that they had invented the account. He could never get the two to agree with him.

Simon: Was that operating room in the hospital blue?

Barney: No, it was bright lights.

Simon: Did you feel that you were going to be operated on?

Barney: No.

Simon: Did you feel that you were being attacked in any way?

Barney: No.[2]

During another session Simon tried again to trip up Barney.

Simon: Just a minute. Didn't Betty tell this to you while you were asleep?

Barney: No. Betty never told me this. . . .

Simon: Yes, but didn't she tell you that you were taken inside?

Barney: Yes, she did.

Simon: Then she told you everything that was seen inside and about being stopped by these men?

Barney: No. She did not tell me about being stopped by the men. She did not have this in her dreams.[3]

At another point, Simon suggested to Barney that the incident could have been a hallucination. Barney disagreed.

The accuracy of abduction accounts depends, to a large degree, upon the skill and competence of the hypnotist. Memory is fallible and there are many influences that prevent its precision. Hypnosis, properly conducted and cautiously used, can be a useful and accurate tool for uncovering abduction memories. Competent hypnosis can illuminate the origin of false memories and can untangle the web of confusing memories. What emerges are accurate, consistent, richly detailed, corroborated accounts of abductions that unlock their secrets and add to our knowledge of them.

Notes

1. For a short discussion of some of my hypnosis techniques, see David M. Jacobs and Budd Hopkins, "Suggested Techniques for Hypnosis and Therapy of Abductees," *Journal of UFO Studies*, New Series, vol. 4, 1992, pp. 138–51. A revised version of this article is available to qualified therapists and researchers. For an excellent survey of abduction critiques, see Stuart Appelle, "The Abduction Experience: A Critical Evaluation of Theory and Evidence," *Journal of UFO Studies*, vol. 6, 1995/1996, pp. 29–79.

2. John Fuller, *The Interrupted Journey* (New York: The Dial Press, 1966), pp. 122–23.

3. Fuller, p. 198.

Corroborating Evidence Supports Hypnotic Recall of Alien Abductions

Budd Hopkins

Corroborating evidence has been found to support claims of alien abduction. Some abductions have eyewitness testimony; some abductees have scars to back up their reports of medical experimentation; physical traces have been found on the ground where alien spaceships have landed; and photographs have been taken of unknown objects in the sky. In addition, accounts of alien abduction are remarkably similar in specific details that are little known by the general public. Budd Hopkins, an artist, is director of the Intruders Foundation and a noted alien abduction researcher. He is the author of several books about alien abductions, including *Missing*

Time; Intruders: The Incredible Visitations at Copley Woods; and Witnessed: The True Story of the Brooklyn Bridge Abductions.

Critics are fond of remarking that there should be corroborating outside evidence to support material that is recovered hypnotically. I agree and will go even further: there should be corroborating evidence to support nonhypnotic testimony, too, whether we are dealing with police work, clinical hypnotherapy, or UFO abduction accounts. I will therefore present several categories of evidence that support the physical reality of specific abduction cases. Familiarity with at least some of these complex cases is essential to an understanding of the reasons many UFO investigators regard abductions as actual, rather than "imaginal," events.

Eyewitness Testimony

Although this kind of confirmation is quite rare, as a result of an extensive, years-long investigation of the 1989 Linda Cortile abduction case, I obtained testimony from four eyewitnesses who, at two different locations, saw Cortile and three small alien figures float out of a twelfth-floor apartment window and then rise up into a hovering UFO.[1] Two other witnesses at separate locations saw the circular craft, though not the small floating figures. Another witness, at yet another location, saw the courtyard of Cortile's apartment building lit by an unusual light shining down from above at a time consistent with the other reports.

In the 1975 Travis Walton abduction case, six tree cutters, moments before driving away from the scene in panic, saw a blue bolt of light from a hovering UFO hit Walton and lift him a few feet above the ground.[2] When they returned minutes later to search for their companion, he had disappeared. Five days later he reappeared, dehydrated and dis-oriented, consciously recalling a UFO abduction. The re-sults of a series of polygraph tests showed that none of the witnesses revealed any signs of deception. Nevertheless, cer-tain debunkers, insisting that Walton and at least seven other people must have perpetrated an elaborate hoax, pre-sented a mélange of theories and imagined motives but ab-solutely no evidence to support their hypothesis.[3] Another round of polygraph tests administered twenty years after the original event again found that Walton and the original wit-nesses showed no signs of deception.

Physical Marks on Abductees' Bodies

UFO investigators have encountered many kinds of scars, fresh lesions, bruises, and other anomalous marks on the persons of those reporting UFO abductions. The most com-mon type—a "scoop mark"—is a small round or oval de-pression that looks as if it might be the result of the removal of a flesh sample. Scoop marks range from roughly one to two centimeters in diameter and from two to five millime-ters in depth, and they generally appear on the subject's leg or arm. Over the years I have seen dozens of such strikingly similar marks and have photographed many of them.

The second type of lesion is a straight-line cut, from one to nine centimeters in length, and is also often found on the subject's arm or leg. As with scoop marks, one can only speculate about the purpose of such incisions. I have also seen scores of these marks, some of which can be quite dis-figuring.

There are many compelling reasons why investigators of-ten associate such injuries with abduction experiences. First, the subject usually does not consciously remember what caused the wound—only its sudden appearance after a par-tially recalled UFO encounter of some kind. As an example, on 17 April 1989 a North Carolina woman left her bed to get a drink of water and, after a period of "missing time," found herself coming to conscious awareness on the floor of her kitchen.[4] She remembered "hands" pressing her down. Frightened and confused, she returned to bed, and in the morning her guest noticed a fresh 3.5-inch incision near the woman's right shoulder blade. The cut was surrounded with a wide bruise. There was no trace of blood on her skin, her nightgown, the sheets or pillowcases, nor upon the floor. Two days later her physician pronounced the wound a "surgical incision" and could not believe that she had not recalled receiving it. (Predictably, a debunker later theorized that it must have been self-inflicted, even though stabbing oneself in the back probably requires more dexterity than this individual possesses.)

Physical Traces on the Ground

In my book *Intruders* I published photographs and a laboratory analysis of an eight-foot-diameter circle of dead grass and pale, desiccated soil that Kathie Davis believed was the result of a UFO landing in the abduction experience she recalled.[5] Extending outward from this affected area was a three-foot-wide, forty-nine-foot-long straight swath of similarly desiccated soil that ended in an almost geometrically perfect arc. The unaffected surrounding area was quite dark and moist from recent rainstorms. Over the next several years the grass slowly grew from the perimeter inward, gradually breaking down the apparently heat-altered, rocklike soil. In the winter the snow melted more quickly over the dehydrated, hardened material than over the surrounding unaffected areas.

In the 1971 Delphos, Kansas, case, a similar alleged UFO landing area—a doughnut-shaped hollow ring—was described by newspaper reporter Thaddia Smith as follows:

> The circle was still very distinct . . . the soil was dry and crusted. The circle or ring was approximately eight feet across, the [unaffected] center and outside area were still muddy from recent rains. The area of the ring that was dry was . . . very light in color. The object had crushed a dead tree to the ground . . . and from its appearance had broken a limb of a live tree when it landed.[6]

Investigator Ted Phillips has compiled over two thousand such reports of the apparent physical effects of landed UFOs upon the immediate environment.[7] The famous 1981 Trans-en-Provence UFO landing report was investigated thoroughly by GEPAN, a scientific subcommittee of the French version of NASA.[8] In a closely reasoned, sixty-six-page report, the group found that something extraordinary, possibly technological, had interacted with the soil and plants.

Photographic Evidence

Over the decades, scores of photographs, videotapes, and film segments showing unknown objects in the sky—flying or standing still—have been studied by scientists and trained photo analysts such as optical physicist Bruce Maccabee. Although in this area there admittedly are many hoaxes, there also are many photographs, films, and videotapes consistent with witness descriptions of the large, unknown craft they claim to have seen, photographed, and deemed authentic after thorough examination by scientists and photo analysts.[9]

To summarize, hundreds upon hundreds of alleged UFO abduction recollections are supported by corroborating and confluent evidence of various kinds: eyewitness testimony; a repeated pattern of physical scars and lesions that suddenly appear upon the bodies of subjects reporting abductions; similar effects on the soil and vegetation at the site of alleged UFO landings associated with abduction accounts; and photographs, videotapes, and films of UFOs that establish the physical reality of the alleged abduction vehicles.

One of the most frustrating obstacles to the intelligent discussion of the UFO abduction phenomenon—one that precedes any talk of hypnosis—is the fact that most experimental and many clinical psychologists show a nearly complete lack of knowledge of the subject. For example, psychologists Michael Ross and Ian Newby make the following assertion: "There is no physical evidence that the abduction episodes occurred; the lack of films, pictures or telltale marks on individuals or the landscape obviates the possibility of an external reality check."[10] This is not a casual, offhand remark, where its naïveté might be excusable; rather, it appears in their contribution to *Psychological Inquiry*. Although Ross and Newby—along with two dozen other academics and clinicians—were making what they believed to be an intelligent contribution to this special abduction issue of *Psychological Inquiry*, their ill-informed comment about the lack of corroborating evidence is sadly representative of most of their colleagues. The reference list at the end of the article is one of three in the journal that does not include a single book or article presenting abduction case material. Believing that the UFO abduction phenomenon is, on its face, "impossible," these authors seem to feel no need either to interview subjects claiming abduction experiences or to familiarize themselves with the abduction literature. Had they bothered to do either, they would not have made such an egregious factual error. Thus, with little or no information about the physical evidence supporting the reality of UFO abductions, they were apparently content merely to cite various comfortable psychosocial etiologies in order to believe they have solved the mystery.

Further, it should always be remembered that any evidence that supports the physical reality of large, maneuvering, intelligently controlled craft of unknown origin—the

UFOs themselves—opens the door to the *possibility* of the UFO abduction phenomenon. If such UFOs exist, one cannot reject the possibility of UFO abductions.

Unfortunately, the limitations of this viewpoint preclude the discussion of the vast body of evidence supporting the physical reality of UFOs (in addition to the evidence previously cited in support of UFO abductions) beyond mentioning the hundreds of cases in which UFOs are seen visually and simultaneously on radar; the sighting reports by highly trained astronauts like Gordon Cooper, James McDivitt, and Deke Slayton; by astronomers such as Clyde Tombaugh, the discoverer of Pluto; and by hundreds of airline pilots and air traffic controllers over the past fifty years.[11] Any psychosocial explanation of the abduction phenomenon must also consider this basic material. . . .

To summarize, hundreds of powerful, detailed, coherent abduction accounts exist in which hypnosis was never used. Thus the abduction phenomenon cannot be seen as an artifact of hypnosis. In many cases in which hypnosis is used, extensive physical evidence and independent corroborative witness accounts support the event-level reality of the experiences thus elicited. Finally, based on recent experimental evidence, hypnosis does not reliably produce more false memories than can be produced in nonhypnotic situations.

Notes

1. Budd Hopkins, *Witnessed: The True Story of the Brooklyn Bridge Abductions* (New York: Pocket Books, 1996).

2. Jerome Clark, *The UFO Encyclopedia*, 2 vols. (Detroit: Omnigraphics, 1998).

3. Philip J. Klass, *UFO Abductions: A Dangerous Game* (Buffalo, N.Y.: Prometheus Books, 1988).

4. Hopkins, case files.

5. B. Hopkins, *Intruders: The Incredible Visitations at Copley Woods* (New York: Random House, 1987).

6. T. Phillips, "Landing Report from Delphos," *FSR Case Histories* 9 (February 1972): 4–10.

7. T. Phillips, "Physical Trace Landing Reports: The Case for UFOs," in *MUFON 1985 UFO Symposium Proceedings*, ed. W. Andrus and R. Hall (Seguin, Tex.: Mutual UFO Network, 1985).

8. J.-J. Velasco, "Report on the Analysis of Anomalous Physical Traces: The 1981 Trans-en-Provence UFO Case," *Journal of Scientific Exploration* 4, no. 1 (1990): 27–48.

9. O. Fontes, "The UAO Sightings at the Island of Trindade, Pt. 1," *APRO Bulletin* (January 1960): 5–9; "Pt. 2" (March 1960): 5–8; "Pt. 3" (May 1960): 4–8; B. Macabbee, "The McMinnville Photos," in *The Spectrum of UFO Research: The Proceedings of the Second CUFOS Conference, Held September 25–27, 1981, in Chicago, Illinois*, ed. M. Hynek (Chicago: J. Allen Hynek Center for UFO Studies, 1988), pp. 13–57.

10. Michael Ross and Ian Newby, "Target Article: Toward an Explanation of the UFO Abduction Phenomenon," *Psychological Inquiry* 7 (1994): 175.

11. D. Berliner, M. Galbraith, and A. Huneeus, *Unidentified Flying Objects: Briefing Document: The Best Available Evidence* (Washington, D.C.: CUFOS, FUFOR, MUFON, 1995); R. Hall, *The UFO Evidence* (New York: Barnes and Noble, 1997).

An Alien Encounter

Bill Chalker

Bill Chalker is a chemist and noted ufologist in Australia. In the following selection, he describes an unusual event that happened to Nobel laureate Kary Mullis at his cabin in the woods in northern California. Mullis was walking in the dark with a flashlight when he was greeted by a glowing raccoon who spoke to him. The next thing Mullis remembers is walking along a road several hours later without his flashlight. He discovers he has an inexplicable feeling of fear and dread in a part of his woods which lasts until he takes out his feelings of anger and frustration by shooting a rifle at the trees. Mullis later discovers that his daughter and a friend had similar experiences when they visited his cabin. Although Mullis is unable to duplicate his experience or perform any tests, he nevertheless knows what happened to him and others was real.

*E*ditor's Note: *This article is a supplement to Bill Chalker's* "Strange Evidence" *published in the Spring 1999* International UFO Reporter, *which recounts the details of an Australian ab-*

duction case that yielded a strand of apparent alien hair suitable for mitochondrial DNA analysis. The results were surprising, yielding a DNA sequence that was human, though very rare. Here Bill Chalker describes the bizarre experiences of Kary Mullis, winner of the 1993 Nobel Prize in chemistry for his invention of a process that allows scientists to identify a fragment of DNA genetic code and then reproduce it in very large quantities. The DNA procedure described in the IUR article was made possible by Mullis's discovery.

On a Friday night in April 1983, Dr. Kary Mullis, a biochemist, was driving up to his cabin in Mendocino county in northern California. During that drive to his Anderson Valley cabin Mullis conceived one of the great discoveries of modern chemistry—the polymerase chain reaction (PCR), a surprisingly simple method for making unlimited copies of DNA, thereby revolutionizing biochemistry almost overnight. Kary Mullis described his discovery in *Scientific American* ("The Unusual Origin of the Polymerase Chain Reaction," April, 1990). He was awarded the 1993 Nobel Prize in Chemistry for his discovery.

A Strange Experience

On another Friday night, during the summer of 1985, Kary Mullis drove up to his cabin. Arriving around midnight after driving for about three hours, Mullis dumped groceries he bought on the way, switched on the lights (powered by solar batteries) and headed, with flashlight in hand, to the outside toilet located about 50 feet west of the cabin. He never got there that night. Quoting from his 1998 book *Dancing Naked in the Mind Field*, Mullis encountered something extraordinarily weird on the way. ". . . at the far end of the path, under a fir tree, there was something glowing. I pointed my flashlight at it anyhow. It only made it whiter where the beam landed. It seemed to be a raccoon. I wasn't frightened. Later, I wondered if it could have been a holo-gram, projected from God knows where."

"The raccoon spoke. 'Good evening, doctor,' it said. I said something back, I don't remember what, probably, 'Hello.' The next thing I remember, it was early in the morning. I was walking along a road uphill from my house."

Mullis had no idea how he got there but he was not wet from the extensive early morning dew. His flashlight was missing. He was never able to find it. He had no signs of in-jury or bruising. The lights of the cabin were still on, along with the groceries on the floor. Some six hours had gone by unaccounted for. Later in the day he found that an area of his property—"the most beautiful part of my woods"—had inexplicably become a place of dread. A year or so later Mullis exorcised this fear John Wayne–style by shooting the wood up. While his attempt at psychotherapy proved suc-cessful it did not help him find out what had happened that night in the summer of 1985. Mullis would become the only known Nobel prize laureate to claim an experience of what might be an alien abduction.

Kary Mullis describes himself as "a generalist with a chemical prejudice." Others have described him as "Hunter Thompson meets Stephen Hawking" or "the world's most eccentric and outspoken Nobel Prize–winning scientist." It is not easy to dispose of Mullis's experience as a drug or al-coholic hallucination. For one, he was not affected by either that midnight. Plus, he has not been the only one to have experienced strange events at the cabin.

His daughter, Louise, disappeared for about three hours after wandering down the same hill. She also reappeared on the same stretch of road. Her frantic fiancé was about to call the local sheriff. Mullis had told no one of his experience until his daughter called to tell him to buy Whitley Strieber's *Communion*. She was ringing to also tell her father about her strange experience. By coincidence when she rang, Mullis had already been drawn to the book and was up to the point where Strieber reports strange "owls" and little men entering his house.

In his own book Mullis concluded, "I wouldn't try to publish a scientific paper about these things, because I can't do any experiments. I can't make glowing raccoons appear. I can't buy them from a scientific supply house to study. I can't cause myself to be lost again for several hours. But I don't deny what happened. It's what science calls anecdotal, because it only happened in a way that you can't reproduce. But it happened."

The Friend's Story

Kary Mullis confirmed all this and more when I spoke with him recently. Another person encountered a "glowing raccoon" between the cabin and the toilet. This was a friend of Mullis who did not know of the "raccoon" story and was a first-time visitor, during a party at the cabin after the announcement of the Nobel Prize win in 1993. This man did not stick around and fled up the hill towards the house. On the way he encountered a small glowing man, which then suddenly enlarged into a full sized man who said something like, "I'll see you tomorrow." The man, who was not experiencing a drug- or alcohol-induced hallucination left with a friend without informing anyone. They returned to their hotel at a nearby town. That night the man inexplicably found himself outside in the hotel car park troubled and terrified by the impression he had somehow been back at the Mullis cabin. He and his friend returned the following night to the cabin. The celebratory party was carrying on from the previous night. As the man arrived he was shocked to see the "full-sized man" seen as an enlarging apparition the night before drive up in a car. This was too much for the first time visitor. He left in a panic, holding Mullis some-how responsible for the previous night's events. Sometime later in tears he revealed the full story to Mullis, who iden-tified the man his friend he had seen as his elderly neigh-bor. Mullis checked with his neighbor and sure enough he had come to the party on the second night, arriving to be seen by the terrified visitor. However he was certain he was not there on the first night, not in person and not lurking as a glowing raccoon or a small glowing man that enlarged into a vision of himself. There is more but that can perhaps wait for another more detailed telling.

Given this sort of activity on his property it perhaps isn't surprising that Kary Mullis told me he thinks the nature of his experience is even stranger than abducting ETs. Instead he speculates about multi-dimensional physics (a la Michio Kaku's *Hyperspace*, 1994) at a macrocosmic level, "like any-thing can god-damn happen and the speed of light is not really the limit in terms of interactions with other cultures or whatever. This stuff about grabbing people or subjecting them to all kinds of experiments—it's just anthropology at a level we don't understand quite yet." As for PCR testing of biological samples from abductee experiences he indicated, "You might imagine that I thought of that myself. As for in-stance in 'you can have some of mine, if I can have some of yours.'" He would like to look at this work, however he feels that the idea of an alien culture needing our DNA to survive is very unlikely and a program on the scale and nature of David Jacobs's *The Threat* improbable. [Jacobs believes that aliens are abducting humans to produce a hybrid species to take over Earth.] Any culture that could conquer the barrier of space-time could have easily conquered the far simpler problems of complex biochemistry and would not need us in the manner described in the grey alien-human "hybrid" agenda theories.

Chapter 2

Fact or Fiction?

The Evidence Against Alien Abductions

It Is Unlikely That Humans Are Abducted by Aliens

Michael Shermer

Michael Shermer, publisher of *Skeptic* magazine, is the director of the Skeptics Society. He is the author of *Denying History* and *Why People Believe Weird Things: Pseudoscience, Superstition, and Other Confusions of Our Time*. In the following selection, he describes an experience in which he believed aliens had taken over the bodies of his friends. However, he was extremely sleep deprived at the time and was hallucinating. Although he realizes it was a hallucination, the memory is still very clear and strong in his mind. He believes that other accounts of alien abductions are influenced by hypnosis, hallucinations, and sleep paralysis.

On Monday, August 8, 1983, I was abducted by aliens. It was late at night and I was traveling along a lonely rural

67

highway approaching the small town of Haigler, Nebraska, when a large craft with bright lights hovered alongside me and forced me to stop. Alien creatures got out and cajoled me into their vehicle. I do not remember what happened inside but when I found myself traveling back down the road I had lost ninety minutes of time. Abductees call this "missing time," and my abduction a "close encounter of the third kind." I'll never forget the experience, and, like other abductees, I've recounted my abduction story numerous times on television and countless times to live audiences.

A Personal Abduction Experience

This may seem like a strange story for a skeptic to be telling, so let me fill in the details. For many years I competed as a professional ultra-marathon bicycle racer, primarily focusing on the 3,000-mile, nonstop, transcontinental Race Across America. "Nonstop" means racers go long stretches without sleep, riding an average of twenty-two out of every twenty-four hours. It is a rolling experiment on stress, sleep deprivation, and mental breakdown.

Under normal sleep conditions, most dream activity is immediately forgotten or fades fairly soon after waking into consciousness. Extreme sleep deprivation breaks down the wall between reality and fantasy. You have severe hallucinations that seem as real as the sensations and perceptions of daily life. The words you hear and speak are recalled like a normal memory. The people you see are as corporeal as those in real life.

During the inaugural 1982 race, I slept three hours on each of the first two nights and consequently fell behind the leader, who was proving that one could get by with considerably less sleep. By New Mexico, I began riding long stretches without sleep in order to catch up, but I was not prepared for the hallucinations that were to come. Mostly they were the garden-variety hallucinations often experienced by weary truck drivers, who call the phenomenon "white-line fever": bushes form into lifelike animals, cracks in the road make meaningful designs, and mailboxes look like people. I saw giraffes and lions. I waved to mailboxes. I even had an out-of-body experience near Tucumcari, New Mexico, where I saw myself riding on the shoulder of Interstate 40 from above.

Hallucination

Finishing third that year, I vowed to ride sleepless in 1983 until I got the lead or collapsed. Eighty-three hours away from the Santa Monica Pier, just shy of Haigler, Nebraska, and 1,259 miles into the race, I was falling asleep on the bike so my support crew (every rider has one) put me down for a forty-five-minute nap. When I awoke I got back on my bike, but I was still so sleepy that my crew tried to get me back into the motorhome. It was then that I slipped into some sort of altered state of consciousness and became convinced that my entire support crew were aliens from another planet and that they were going to kill me. So clever were these aliens that they even looked, dressed, and spoke like my crew. I began to quiz individual crew members about details from their personal lives and about the bike that no alien should know. I asked my mechanic if he had glued on my bike tires with spaghetti sauce. When he replied that he had glued them on with Clement glue (also red), I was quite impressed with the research the aliens had done. Other questions and correct answers followed. The context for this hallucination was a 1960s television program—*The Invaders*—in which the aliens looked exactly like humans with the exception of a stiff little finger. I looked for stiff pinkies on my crew members. The motorhome with its bright lights became their spacecraft. After the crew managed to bed me down for another forty-five minutes, I awoke clear-headed and the problem was solved. To this day, however, I recall the hallucination as vividly and clearly as any strong memory.

Now, I am not claiming that people who have had alien abduction experiences were sleep deprived or undergoing extreme physical and mental stress. However, I think it is fairly clear that if an alien abduction experience can happen under these conditions, it can happen under other conditions. Obviously I was not abducted by aliens, so what is more likely: that other people are having experiences similar to mine, triggered by other altered states and unusual circumstances, or that we really are being visited secretly by aliens from other worlds? By Scottish philosopher David Hume's criterion of how to judge a miracle—"no testimony is sufficient to establish a miracle, unless the testimony be of such a kind, that its falsehood would be more miraculous than the fact which it endeavors to establish"—we would have to choose the first explanation. It is not impossible that aliens are traveling thousands of light years to Earth and dropping in undetected, but it is much more likely that humans are experiencing altered states of consciousness and interpreting them in the context of what is popular in our culture today, namely, space aliens. . . .

Encounters with Alien Abductees

In 1994 NBC began airing *The Other Side*, a New Age show that explored alien abduction claims, as well as other mysteries, miracles, and unusual phenomena. I appeared numerous times on this show as the token skeptic, but most interesting for me was their two-part program on UFOs and alien abductions. The claims made by the alien abductees were quite remarkable indeed. They state that literally millions of people have been "beamed up" to alien spacecraft, some straight out of their bedrooms through walls and ceilings. One woman said the aliens took her eggs for use in a breeding experiment but could produce no evidence for how this was done. Another said that the aliens actually implanted a human-alien hybrid in her womb and that she gave birth to the child. Where is this child now? The aliens took it back, she explained. One man pulled up his pant leg to show me scars on his legs that he said were left by the aliens. They looked like normal scars to me. Another woman said the aliens had implanted a tracking device in her head, much as biologists do to track dolphins or birds. An MRI of her head proved negative. One man explained that the aliens took his sperm. I asked him how he knew that they took his sperm, since he had said he was asleep when he was abducted. He said he knew because he had had an orgasm. I responded, "Is it possible you simply had a wet dream?" He was not amused.

After the taping of this program, about a dozen of the "abductees" were going out to dinner. Since I tend to be a fairly friendly, nonconfrontational skeptic in these situations, disdaining the shouting so desired by talk-show producers, they invited me to join them. It was enlightening. I discovered that they were neither crazy nor ignorant, as one might suspect. They were perfectly sane, rational, intelligent folks who had in common an irrational experience. They were convinced of the reality of the experience—no rational explanation I could offer, from hallucinations to lucid dreams to false memories, could convince them otherwise. One man became teary-eyed while telling me how traumatic the abduction was for him. Another woman explained that the experience had cost her a happy marriage to a wealthy television producer. I thought, "What is wrong here? There isn't a shred of evidence that any of these claims are true, yet these are normal, rational folks whose lives have been deeply affected by these experiences."

In my opinion, the alien abduction phenomenon is the product of an unusual altered state of consciousness interpreted in a cultural context replete with films, television programs, and science fiction literature about aliens and UFOs. Add to this the fact that for the past four decades we have been exploring the solar system and searching for signs of extraterrestrial intelligence, and it is no wonder that people are seeing UFOs and experiencing alien encounters. Driven by mass media that revel in such tabloid-type stories, the alien abduction phenomenon is now in a positive feedback loop. The more people who have had these unusual mental experiences see and read about others who have interpreted similar incidents as abduction by aliens, the more likely it is that they will convert their own stories into their own alien abduction. The feedback loop was given a strong boost in late 1975 after millions watched NBC's *The UFO Incident,* a movie on Betty and Barney Hill's abduction dreams. The stereotypical alien with a large, bald head and big, elongated eyes, reported by so many abductees since 1975, was created by NBC artists for this program. The rate of information exchange took off as more and more alien abductions were reported on the news and recounted in popular books, newspapers, tabloids, and specialty publications dedicated solely to UFOs and alien abductions. As there seemed to be agreement on how the aliens looked and also on their preoccupation with human reproductive systems (usually women are sexually molested by the aliens), the feedback loop took off. Because of our fascination with the possibility of extraterrestrial life, and there is a real possibility that extraterrestrials might exist somewhere in the cosmos (a different question than their arrival here on Earth), this craze will probably wax and wane depending on what is hot in pop culture. Blockbuster films like *ET* and *Independence Day* and television shows like *Star Trek* and *The X-Files*, as well as best-selling books like Whitley Strieber's *Communion* and John Mack's *Abduction*, continue feeding the movement.

The Role of Hypnosis

While dining with the abductees, I found out something very revealing: not one of them recalled being abducted immediately after the experience. In fact, for most of them, many years went by before they "remembered" the experience. How was this memory recalled? Under hypnosis. . . . Memories cannot simply be "recovered" like rewinding a videotape. Memory is a complex phenomenon involving distortions, deletions, additions, and sometimes complete fabrication. Psychologists call this *confabulation*—mixing fantasy with reality to such an extent that it is impossible to sort them out. Psychologist Elizabeth Loftus (Loftus and Ketcham 1994) has shown how easy it is to plant a false memory in a child's mind by merely repeating a suggestion until the child incorporates it as an actual memory. Similarly, Professor Alvin Lawson put students at California State University, Long Beach, into a hypnotic state and in their altered state told them over and over that they had been abducted by aliens. When asked to fill in the details of the abduction, the students elaborated in great detail, making it up as they went along in the story (in Sagan 1996). Every parent has stories about the fantasies their children create. My daughter once described to my wife a purple dragon we saw on our hike in the local hills that day.

True, not all abduction stories are recalled only under hypnosis, but almost all alien abductions occur late at night during sleep. In addition to normal fantasies and lucid dreams, there are rare mental states known as *hypnogogic hallucinations*, which occur soon after falling asleep, and *hypnopompic hallucinations,* which happen just before waking up. In these unusual states, subjects report a variety of experiences, including floating out of their bodies, feeling paralyzed, seeing loved ones who have passed away, witnessing ghosts and poltergeists, and, yes, being abducted by aliens. Psychologist Robert A. Baker presents as typical this subject's report: "I went to bed and went to sleep and then sometime near morning something woke me up. I opened my eyes and found myself wide awake but unable to move. There, standing at the foot of my bed was my mother, wearing her favorite dress—the one we buried her in" (1987/1988, p. 157). Baker also demonstrates that Whitley Strieber's encounter with aliens (one of the more famous in abduction lore) "is a classic, textbook description of a hypnopompic hallucination, complete with awakening from a sound sleep, the strong sense of reality and of being awake, the paralysis (due to the fact that the body's neural circuits keep our muscles relaxed and help preserve our sleep), and the encounter with strange beings" (p. 157).

Harvard psychiatrist John Mack, a Pulitzer Prize–winning author, gave the abduction movement a strong endorsement with his 1994 book, *Abduction: Human Encounters with Aliens.* Here at last was a mainstream scholar from a highly respectable institution lending credence (and his reputation) to the belief in the reality of these encounters. Mack was impressed by the commonalities of the stories told by abductees—the physical description of the aliens, the sexual abuse, the metallic probes, and so on. Yet I think we can expect consistencies in the stories since so many of the abductees go to the same hypnotist, read the same alien encounter books, watch the same science fiction movies, and in many cases even know one another and belong to "encounter" groups (in both senses of the word). Given the shared mental states and social contexts, it would be surprising if there was not a core set of characteristics of the abduction experience shared by the abductees. And what are we to do with the shared absence of convincing physical evidence?

The Sexual Component

Finally, the sexual component of alien abduction experiences demands comment. It is well known among anthropologists and biologists that humans are the most sexual of all primates, if not all mammals. Unlike most animals, when it comes to sex, humans are not constrained by biological rhythms and the cycle of the seasons. We like sex almost anytime or anywhere. We are stimulated by visual sexual cues, and sex is a significant component in advertising, films, television programs, and our culture in general. You might say we are obsessed with sex. Thus, the fact that alien abduction experiences often include a sexual encounter tells us more about humans than it does about aliens. . . . Women in the sixteenth and seventeenth centuries were often accused of (and even allegedly experienced or confessed to) having illicit sexual encounters with aliens—in this case the alien was usually Satan himself—and these women were burned as witches. In the nineteenth century, many people reported sexual encounters with ghosts and spirits at about the time that the spiritualism movement took off in England and America. And in the twentieth century, we have phenomena such as "Satanic ritual abuse," in which children and young adults are allegedly being sexually abused in cult rituals; "recovered memory syndrome," in which adult women and men are "recovering" memories of sexual abuse that allegedly occurred decades previously; and "facilitated communication," where autistic children are "communicating" through facilitators (teachers or parents) who hold the child's hand above a typewriter or computer keyboard reporting that they were sexually abused.

We can again apply Hume's maxim: is it more likely that demons, spirits, ghosts, and aliens have been and continue to sexually abuse humans or that humans are experiencing fantasies and interpreting them in the social context of their age and culture? I think it can reasonably be argued that such experiences are a very earthly phenomenon with a perfectly natural (albeit unusual) explanation. To me, the fact that humans have such experiences is at least as fascinating and mysterious as the possibility of the existence of extraterrestrial intelligence.

Bibliography

Baker, R.A. 1987/1988. The Aliens Among Us: Hypnotic Regression Revisited. *Skeptical Inquirer* 12, no. 2:147–162.

Sagan, C. 1996. *The Demon Haunted World: Science as a Candle in the Dark.* New York: Random House.

Alien Abductions Are Really Sleep Paralysis

Joe Nickell

The phenomenon of alien abduction can be attributed to a dream-like state. Many so-called abductees relate how they woke up from a deep sleep and could not move, a common experience known as sleep paralysis. Other accounts of alien abduction are clearly examples of waking dreams, in which the subject is not quite asleep and not quite awake. Sleep paralysis and waking dreams have been responsible for reports of nightly visitations from strange creatures since the Middle Ages. Joe Nickell is a senior research fellow at the Committee for the Scientific Investigation of Claims of the Paranormal.

In his latest book, *The Communion Letters* (1997), self-claimed alien abductee Whitley Strieber, assisted by his wife

Joe Nickell, "Alien Abductions as Sleep-Related Phenomena," *Skeptical Inquirer*, May/June 1998, pp. 16–19. Copyright © 1998 by *Skeptical Inquirer*. Reproduced by permission.

Ann, offers a selection of letters Strieber has received in response to his various alien-abduction books, particularly the bestselling *Communion: A True Story* (1987). A careful analysis of these letters is illuminating.

The sixty-seven narratives making up *The Communion Letters* represent, the Striebers claim, what "could conceivably be the first true communication from another world that has ever been recorded." Selected from nearly two hundred thousand letters, the collection, they assert, "will put certain shibboleths to rest forever," namely that the phenomenon is limited to a few people, that they are alone when abducted, that the events are recalled only under hypnosis, and that the abductees are attention-seekers (Strieber and Strieber 1997, 3–4).

Be that as it may, the accounts are really surprising for their prevalence of simple, well-understood, sleep-related phenomena. Most, for example, include one or more experiences that can easily be attributed to some type of dream.

The Waking Dream

Clearly the dominant phenomenon in the accounts—albeit one little known to the public—is the common "waking dream." This occurs when the subject is in the twilight state between waking and sleeping, and combines features of both. Such dreams typically include perception of bright lights or other bizarre imagery, such as apparitions of strange creatures. Auditory hallucinations are also possible. Waking dreams are termed hypnagogic hallucinations if the subject is going to sleep, or hypnopompic if he or she is awakened (Drever 1971, 125). Frequently the latter is accompanied by what is known as sleep paralysis, an inability to move caused by the body remaining in the sleep mode.

In the middle ages, waking dreams were often responsible for reports of demons (incubuses and succubuses) which, due to sleep paralysis, sometimes seemed to be sitting on the percipient's chest or lying atop his or her body. At other times, waking dreams have been common sources of "ghosts," "angels," and other imagined entities (Nickell 1995). Now, as the collection of letters to the Striebers demonstrates, these experiences are producing "aliens" and related imagery. Some forty-two of the sixty-seven narratives include one or more apparent waking dreams.

For example, one man wrote: "I'd wake up and my heart would be pounding as if I was frightened. I'd also see two white lights, one slightly higher than the other, flying or floating across my room in a descending motion toward the floor. . . . I would have what I called a 'dream,' although I felt that I was totally awake because I could move my eyes. My body would be completely paralyzed. I couldn't yell or scream, but wanted to" (p. 87). Another man reported: "At night, after my parents would put me to bed, I'd often see small, very white round faces with huge black eyes staring in at me from outside my bedroom window. Sometimes it was only one, but often it was several. . . . I saw them several nights a week almost into my teens" (p. 37). Still another man wrote: "When I was twenty-three I woke up one night to find a little gray man on the other side of my room. He looked about four feet tall and had very large orange cat eyes. I later learned that this was my 'guardian'" (p. 135).

Although, as these accounts show, some of the "abductees" do not report paralysis, others describe that effect without imagery. For example, one writes: " . . . I woke up into one of the strangest experiences of my life. I was awake, could feel and could smell and think and reason, but I could not see. . . . I experimented with every part of my body to see if I could move; I couldn't. There was a flashlight a few inches from my head, but I couldn't make my arm respond to my mental commands" (p. 40).

Sleep Paralysis

Indeed, sleep paralysis accompanying a waking dream may well be a major factor in convincing some "abductees" they have been examined by aliens. Consider this woman's account:

> I often found myself being awakened in the deepest night by a feeling of someone touching me: pushing my stomach; poking my arms and legs; touching my head and neck; what felt like a breast exam and a heaviness across my chest, and someone holding my feet. This seemed to go on for three nights. On the last night, I vaguely saw, in my efficiency apartment, a "little man" running to and around my refrigerator. My door was always locked, as were the two windows.
>
> Then one night I woke up to find myself in a strange room, strapped to a table, with my feet up. I felt that my lower half was undressed. . . . On another later night, I woke up strapped to a table in a reclining position. (pp. 250–51)

Another phenomenon reported in *The Communion Letters* is the out-of-body experience (OBE). This may be associated with a waking dream, as in this woman's account:

> When I was nineteen I had my first OBE. . . . I should say here that, to my knowledge, all my hundreds of OBEs throughout the years have been conscious ones, meaning that they've all occurred in the state just before sleep, where I am fully conscious and aware of the paralysis, the vibrations that occur, and of the actual separation. . . . On the night of March 15, 1989, I went to bed and fell asleep normally. Sometime during the night I awakened to find myself softly bumping against the ceiling, already separated from the physical. . . . I felt myself being turned around. I 'saw' a being standing in the middle of the open room, approximately fifteen feet away. A telepathic voice asked if I was afraid.

The woman goes on to describe a stereotypical alien (pp. 73–74).

Such "telepathic" voices—which are often part of a waking dream—are, of course, the person's own. Even abduction guru David Jacobs admits that reports of telepathic communication with aliens may be nothing more than confabulation (the tendency of ordinary people to confuse fact with fantasy [Baker and Nickell 1992, 217]). Says Jacobs, "Abductees sometimes slip into a 'channeling' mode—in which the abductee 'hears' messages from his own mind and thinks they are coming from outside sources—and the researcher fails to catch it" (Jacobs 1998, 56).

Out-of-Body Experiences

No fewer than 18 letters in the Strieber collection describe one or more OBEs—or such related phenomena as "astral travel" or floating or flying dreams. The relationship between OBEs and sleep paralysis is demonstrated by a percipient who had "the strangest type of dream" up to three times a week. He would awaken to hear crackling noises followed by a loud boom, "at which point," he says, "I would immediately go into paralysis. Then I would slowly begin to float toward my ceiling, unable to move a limb" (p. 130).

In a few instances the "abductee" is not in bed when the (apparent) waking dream occurs. He or she may be watching television, riding in a car, or—as in the case of one woman—sitting with her child in a rocking chair: "We must have rocked for twenty minutes, and I was actually becoming drowsy. My eyes were closed. Then an odd thing happened: I got a vision of three 'grays' standing in front of the rocking chair. It was as if I could see through my eyelids" (p. 17). The salient point is that the waking dream may occur virtually anywhere—as long as the person is in the state between waking and sleeping.

In fact, the subject may have similar experiences to those in waking dreams when he or she is simply exhausted—i.e., suffering from mental or physical fatigue (Baker 1992, 273). Such might be the explanation for eight reports, like that of one woman who told the Striebers:

> I was going home from work [i.e., presumably tired], and in
> the middle of the Seventh Avenue subway rush hour crowd I
> saw a little man about four feet tall. He had a huge head, but
> it was the quality of his skin that first caught my attention. It
> didn't look like human skin, but more like plastic or rubber.
> I knew he wasn't human. I tried to follow him with my eyes,
> but he quickly got lost in the crowd. No one else seemed to
> notice. This disturbed me; I thought I was seeing things.

This person also had "recurrent dreams" of "spaceships
hovering over the Hudson River and the Palisades. These
dreams were always very vivid and powerful" (p. 207).

Other accounts in *The Communion Letters* clearly indicate
ordinary dreaming, nightmares, "lucid" dreams (vivid, con-
trollable dreams that occur when one is fully asleep), and
the like—in all, reports by some twenty-two letter writers. At
least four reports almost certainly involved somnambulism
(walking or performing other activities while asleep). The
letters also reported "near-death experiences" (two writers)
and hypnosis (another two instances). A majority of the
narratives contain more than one phenomenon, but in all
at least fifty-nine of the sixty-seven letters consist of one or
more instances of probable sleep-related phenomena such
as discussed thus far. (In addition there were such reported
conditions as migraines, panic attacks, post-traumatic syndrome disorder, even schizophrenia—one example of each.
As many as eight people had a number of traits associated
with what is termed "fantasy proneness.")

Lest it be thought that the eight remaining letters are reports of genuine abductions, I consider three to be extremely
doubtful, raising more questions than they answer and even
containing internal inconsistencies or outright contradictions. Of the other five, two are reports of nothing more than
unexplained knocking sounds and three consist merely of
rather typical UFO sightings (two possibly weather bal-

loons), with one writer specifically stating, "I do not believe that an abductee experience is in my recent history" (p. 180).

Impressionable Readers

Strieber's correspondents have, of course, read his books, *Communion, Transformation,* and *Breakthrough,* and they clearly have been influenced by them. Indeed, one writer's experience with "the visitors"—an alleged abduction— "happened the night after I finished your last book, *Breakthrough*" (p. 144). Another, who has "had plenty of UFO experiences," wrote: "I couldn't get the picture of the being on the *Communion* cover out of my head" (pp. 134–135). A woman stated: "When I saw the cover of *Communion* I felt compelled to buy it. When I began to read it, I felt nauseated, burst into tears, was shaking, and was elated. Most books don't elicit this reaction in me as I read the first few chapters" (p. 148). A policeman wrote: "Frankly the books scare the hell out of me. I did not sleep well for weeks following *Communion*. I again feel very restless after reading *Breakthrough*. I cannot explain this. Tell me I am imagining things" (p. 122). Obviously such correspondents are quite impressionable, to say the least.

Many who wrote did so in response to similar events reported by Strieber. Significantly, Strieber's own abduction claims began with his having a waking dream! According to psychologist Robert A. Baker:

> In Strieber's *Communion* is a classic, textbook description of a hypnopompic hallucination, complete with the awakening from a sound sleep, the strong sense of reality and of being awake, the paralysis (due to the fact that the body's neural circuits keep our muscles relaxed and help preserve our sleep), and the encounter with strange beings. Following the encounter, instead of jumping out of bed and going in search of the strangers he has seen, Strieber typically goes back to sleep. He even reports that the burglar alarm was

still working—proof again that the intruders were mental rather than physical. Strieber also reports an occasion when he awakes and believes that the roof of his house in on fire and that the aliens are threatening his family. Yet his only response to this was to go peacefully back to sleep. Again, clear evidence of a hypnopompic dream. Strieber, of course, is convinced of the reality of these experiences. This too is expected. If he was not convinced of their reality, then the experience would not be hypnopompic or hallucinatory (Baker 1987, 157).

Why some people's waking dreams relate to extraterrestrials and others to different entities depends on the person's expectations, which in turn are influenced by various cultural and psychological factors. Thus given different contexts, a waking dream involving a shadowy image and sleep paralysis may be variously reported: someone sleeping in a "haunted" manor house describes a ghostly figure and is "paralyzed with fear," while another, undergoing a religious transformation, perceives an angel and is "transfixed with awe," while yet another, having read *Communion*, sees an extraterrestrial being and feels "strapped to an examining table."

Reinterpretation of Original Experiences

Many of the communicants in *The Communion Letters* even show a willingness to reinterpret their original experiences in light of what they have since read in Strieber's books. This transformational tendency seems quite strong. One woman, for example, who had "imaginary playmates" as a child in the 1940s now reports to Strieber: "The beings that I saw looked like the ones in your book" (p. 93). Another, who saw an entity during an obvious waking dream, reported that her first reaction after reading *Communion* "was to wonder if, in fact, what I recalled was all that had taken place the night of my experience" (p. 119). Still another, a man who would sometimes "wake up with little gray people around me," admitted: "I never associated them with UFOs. As soon as I'd open my eyes, they'd all run away, right through the walls!" (p. 134). Now that he has read *Communion* he believes he was "manipulated" into buying it. This same person also had a "memory" which "came in the form of a vivid dream" and that involved himself, Strieber, and the aliens. "When I awoke," he reported, "I felt as if you had been looking at me intently" (p. 136). In *The Threat*, David Jacobs even tries to convince his readers they should revise their experiences. He suggests their "ghost" or "guardian angel" experience should be considered possible alien encounters, and that they may therefore be "unaware abductees" (Jacobs 1998, 120).

It is distressing that such simple phenomena as waking dreams, sleep paralysis, and out-of-body hallucinations can be transformed into "close encounters." The mechanism is what psychologists call contagion—the spreading of an idea, behavior, etc. from person to person by means of suggestion (Baker and Nickell 1992, 101). Examples of contagion are the Salem witch hysteria of 1692–1693, the spiritualist craze of the nineteenth century, the UFO furor that began in 1947, and, of course, its sequel, today's alien-encounter delusion, which is aided in dissemination by the mass media.

Perhaps we should not be surprised that those who are hyping belief in extraterrestrial abductions ignore or underestimate the psychological factors. Strieber, for example, is a fiction writer, and Budd Hopkins, who helped boost public interest with his 1981 book *Missing Time*, is an artist. One would think that history professor David Jacobs would profit from mistakes of the past and not help repeat them. Even more curious is the involvement of clinical psychologist Edith Fiore (1989) and psychiatrist John Mack (1994). But both confess they are less interested in the truth or falsity of a given claim than what the individual believes happened, with the resulting significance to therapy and, in the case of Mack, to "the larger culture." (Mack 1994, 382. See also Fiore 1989, 333–34; Jacobs 1998, 48–55.)

All of these abduction promoters have books to offer. Let the buyer beware.

References

Baker, Robert A. 1987. The aliens among us: Hypnotic regression revisited. *Skeptical Inquirer* 12(2): 147–162.

———.1992. *Hidden Memories: Voices and Visions from Within.* Buffalo, N.Y.: Prometheus Books.

Baker, Robert A., and Joe Nickell. 1992. *Missing Pieces: How to Investigate Ghosts, UFOs, Psychics, and Other Mysteries.* Amherst, N.Y.: Prometheus Books.

Drever, James. 1971. *A Dictionary of Psychology.* Baltimore: Penguin Books.

Fiore, Edith. 1989. *Encounters: A Psychologist Reveals Case Studies of Abductions by Extraterrestrials.* New York: Doubleday.

Jacobs, David. 1998. *The Threat.* New York: Simon and Schuster.

Mack, John. 1994. *Abduction: Human Encounters with Aliens.* New York: Scribners.

Nickell, Joe. 1995. *Entities: Angels, Spirits, Demons, and Other Alien Beings.* Amherst, N.Y.: Prometheus Books, pp. 41, 46, 55, 59, 117, 131, 157, 209, 214, 268, 278.

Strieber, Whitley. 1987. *Communion: A True Story.* New York: William Morrow.

Strieber, Whitley, and Ann Strieber. 1997. *The Communion Letters.* New York: HarperPrism.

Hypnosis Is an Unreliable Technique for Examining Claims of Alien Abduction

Robert A. Baker

Well-trained and knowledgeable hypnotists who have worked with people who claim to have been abducted by aliens have discovered that the subjects were quite prone to fantasies and that their abduction experiences were actually inspired by dreams and books they had read. Following an explosion of alleged alien abduction cases in the 1980s, many untrained, amateur hypnotists began contacting abductees and elicited strange accounts of abductions and medical and sexual experimentation. However, a close examination of alleged abductees and the stories they tell during hypnosis finds that a large amount of information contained in their accounts are confabulations—made-up "facts" told as if they were really true. In fact, hypnotists can suggest in their subjects memories of events that never happened. Due to amateur hypnotist-gurus, the lives of many innocent and trusting people are ruined, claims author Robert A. Baker. Baker is a professor emeritus of psychology at the University of Kentucky and the author of *They Call It Hypnosis.*

Since the famous abduction case of Betty and Barney Hill, immortalized by John Fuller in his sensational *The Interrupted Journey* (1966), with an introduction by the Hills' hypnotist, Dr. Benjamin Simon, regressive hypnosis has been the method of choice both for getting at the details of the abduction and for establishing the abduction's authenticity. This is, of course, one of the worst if not the worst misuse of so-called hypnosis. The Hill case was one of the first abductions to gain worldwide publicity and it was one of the first to use hypnotic regression.

The Hill Case

To summarize the case, it seems that the Hills, who had been taking a holiday in Canada, started back home in their automobile to New Hampshire. As they passed near the town of Lancaster, Betty noticed a light in the sky. She called her husband's attention to this light, which was soon joined by another. As they watched these lights, one of them disappeared and the other began to follow their car. After they stopped their car and Betty looked at the light through her binoculars. She saw that it emanated from a large craft or vehicle in the sky. Barney got out and walked toward the vehicle, which had dropped down to tree level. When Barney looked at it through the binoculars he thought he saw a dozen or so people looking back at him from the vehicle.

At this point, Barney panicked and ran back to Betty and the car, and they drove off down the road. Shortly thereafter, they heard a beeping sound and they felt very tired. When they reached home, the Hills recalled that they were about two hours later than they should have been. The following morning Betty called her sister, who suggested that they may have been "irradiated" by the UFO. This fear prompted Betty to go the local library and find the book *The Flying Saucer Conspiracy* by Donald Keyhoe, a confirmed believer that "UFOs are from outer space."

A week after their adventure, Betty wrote a letter to a national UFO organization describing their UFO sighting, but she made no mention of any abduction. Several days later, Betty had a nightmare in which she dreamed that she and Barney had been abducted and taken aboard a flying saucer. According to Betty, she was given an extensive physical exam by the UFO occupants, who seemed particularly interested in her reproductive system.

After receiving Betty's letter, the national UFO organization sent some of their investigators around to interview the Hills. The interviewers asked the Hills about the missing two hours. A few weeks later, Barney visited his physician for ulcers and hypertension. The physician recommended that Barney see a psychiatrist. The psychiatrist recommended that Barney contact Dr. Benjamin Simon, who practiced regressive hypnosis.

The Hypnosis Sessions

Betty accompanied Barney on his first visit because in the meantime she had had several abduction dreams. Dr. Simon was surprised to see Betty as well as Barney, but he quickly realized that Betty needed help as well. Under regressive hypnosis, Dr. Simon found that the Hills had, indeed, seen a bright star-like object, and had been frightened because it seemed like it was following them. Dr. Simon quickly recognized, though, that the abduction tale was only a fantasy. Although Betty and Barney agreed about the trip down from Montreal, they did not agree on details about the alleged abduction, and it became obvious to Dr. Simon that the so-called abduction was not a shared experience. In Fuller's book, this aspect of the case was not emphasized. Neither was the fact that more than two years had elapsed between the time of the UFO encounter and the sessions with Dr. Simon.

When Dr. Simon had Betty bring in notes she had made about her nightmares at the time of the nightmares and compared these with the tale she told under regressive hypnosis, he found that the two were essentially identical. There were irrational inconsistencies in both the abduction story and the notes about her dreams. Dr. Simon has stated, on several occasions, that he does not believe that the Hills were abducted and taken aboard a UFO, but rather, that Betty Hill's memories of the alleged abduction were based solely upon her dreams. Unfortunately, some of the people she told about her dreams suggested to her that her dreams must have been based upon events that actually happened. The truth of the matter seems to be that her dreams were based upon the UFO material supplied by the investigators and the books she had read. Although Barney's recall under hypnotic regression was corroborative in some ways, it must be remembered that Betty had told him over and over for more than two years the content of her dreams.

The Hill case is important because it contained all the main components of future abduction claims: missing time, spatial dislocations, physical isolation from the rest of the world during the event, physical examination inside the UFO, and interest of the aliens in the earthlings' reproductive system. All of these show up time and again in cases of alleged abduction revealed through hypnotic regression.

Following the Hill case, reports of UFO abductions began to proliferate. In October 1973, Charles Hickson and Calvin Parker of Pascagoula, Mississippi, reported they had been abducted and taken aboard a flying saucer for a superficial physical examination. According to them, their abductors were short, grey men with wrinkled skin, and rather than walking, they "floated." UFO experts, after interviewing Hickson and Parker, concluded that they were telling the truth. Claims were even made that Hickson successfully passed a lie detector test supporting his abduction story. A more rigorous investigation by Philip J. Klass (1989) discovered that the case was a hoax, that the lie detector test was flawed, and the abduction a "put-up job" to make money.

Following the 1975 NBC television prime time movie "The UFO Incident," telling the story of Betty and Barney Hill, numerous other claims of abductions were made, including the notorious Travis Walton case. In this case, a group of woodcutters in one of the Arizona national forests was cutting wood when all of a sudden a hovering UFO "zapped" young Walton, one of the workers, and he disappeared. Five days later, Walton reappeared and told of being taken aboard a spaceship and given a physical exam. This case was unique in that there were multiple witnesses and a report to the authorities that was made while the abductee was still missing. There were, however, some discordant elements. First, the abduction occurred only two weeks after the NBC telecast. Second, Walton's older brother Duane assured everyone Travis wasn't even missing. And third, all of the Waltons were UFO buffs, and Travis had told his mother well before the incident that if he were ever abducted she shouldn't worry. Subsequent investigation by Klass again uncovered a monetary motive behind this hoax (Klass 1989).

In the spring of 1979, one of the most incredible UFO

abduction stories of all time appeared in a book titled *The Andreasson Affair: The Documented Investigation of a Woman's Abduction Aboard a UFO*, authored by Raymond Fowler, an experienced UFOlogist. According to Mrs. Andreasson, a Massachusetts mother of seven, in January 1967, only a few months after the Hill abduction gained international attention, she too was abducted. However, it was not until 1974—seven years later—that she decided to go public and attempt to collect the $100,000 prize offered by the tabloid *National Enquirer* for convincing evidence of extraterrestrial visitors. Despite the story she told under regressive hypnosis administered during fourteen separate sessions by one Harold Edelstein, she never collected the prize money. Even Fowler himself had some doubts about some of the bizarre details of Mrs. Andreasson's story. Since none of the details about the strange beings without heads and her visit to another world could possibly be verified, it seems clear that it is another excellent example of the imaginative skill of someone who is fantasy-prone.

The abduction phenomenon reached its peak perhaps during the middle and later 1980s, when a number of claims were reported from all over the planet of numerous UFO contacts and abductions by aliens. In the wake of these claims came another phenomenon: the hypnotic-regression guru, an untrained, nonprofessional, amateur hypnotist specializing in contacting alleged abductees and eliciting strange and spectacular tales of abduction, examination, molestation, impregnation, and surgical implantation.

Budd Hopkins

Typical of such gurus is Budd Hopkins, an artist by profession, who abandoned his trade for the more lucrative work of UFO-abduction propagandist. In his first book on UFO abductions, *Missing Time* (1981), Hopkins describes the adventures of some thirty-seven people from all walks of life who underwent a "missing time" experience and then later, under Hopkins hypnotic ministrations, reported a classic UFO abduction fantasy quite similar to that of Betty and Barney Hill. Hopkins focuses on nineteen individuals, all of whom had body scars, missing time, and memories of alien faces. He stresses that all of the nineteen are normal, and even raises the possibility that their reports of alien abductions might be delusional. All such doubts as to the validity of such abductions were, however, quickly erased when Hopkins followed up his first book with a second one called *Intruders: The Incredible Visitations at Copley Woods* (1987), in which he discovered the motive behind the abductions! It is, incredibly, that the aliens are carrying out an extraterrestrial genetic experiment in which earthlings are unknowing and unwilling participants!

Nearly all of Hopkins's evidence is gathered from alleged victims who have sought him out in the hope that he can explain or explain away their "missing time" or "UFO contact" experiences. With these initial expectations and Hopkins's "hypnotic style," it would be remarkable indeed if anything other than an abduction experience emerged.

The ABC program "20/20" on May 21, 1987, devoted a segment to UFO abductions. Hopkins was interviewed along with a number of other believers. The show also interviewed one skeptic, Dr. Martin Reiser, a psychologist and hypnosis consultant for the Los Angeles Police Department. After viewing videotapes of Hopkins interviewing a subject under hypnosis, Reiser concluded that Hopkins was telling the subjects ahead of time that abductions happen, that they are very common, and that there is no question that the alien abductors do exist. Hopkins's response was, "Well, these cases are so outrageous and the person feels so uncomfortable talking about them that, unless you assure that person by your manner that you believe them, you will not get the story." Reiser responded, "I think much of what was felt and perceived by these two subjects could be explained in rational, reasonable ways that don't have to involve UFOs or UFO experiences."

Whitley Strieber

Hopkins has been out-gurued within the last few years by Whitley Strieber, the occult novelist, whose book *Communion: A True Story* (1987) was on the New York Times best-seller list for nearly a year, and made his publisher, Beech Tree Books/Morrow, a fortune and made Strieber an international celebrity. The book is highly autobiographical and gives an account of Strieber's early life, when he had a number of experiences that he was able, at a much later time, to relate to contacts with extraterrestrials. Some of this biographical material was recovered under hypnosis and is, therefore, highly suspect. Nevertheless, Strieber describes a number of " missing time" episodes, conversations with voices coming through his stereo system, and out-of-the-body experiences.

Things come to a head one night in October 1985, when Strieber is in his isolated cabin in upstate New York with his wife and son and another couple. After everyone is asleep, Strieber awakens and sees a blue light on the cathedral ceiling of the living room. He thinks the house is afire. Though afraid and almost in a state of panic, he goes back to sleep! He is awakened again by a sharp loud noise like a firecracker. His wife and son and the guests also hear it and awaken, and the house is surrounded by a glowing light. Strieber goes downstairs then and the light disappears. He comforts his son and his guests and all go back to sleep. Later, under hypnosis, Strieber remembers being visited during the night by a little man with a hood but no head.

Three months later, on the day after Christmas, Strieber and his wife and son are again in the cabin. After shutting up the cabin, setting the alarm system, and checking the place thoroughly, he falls asleep. Next, he is suddenly awakened by a whooshing noise from downstairs. He checks the alarm system, but there is no indication that there has been any intrusion. Then he sees the bedroom door open, and a small figure about three-and-a-half-feet tall is staring at him. Then he is paralyzed and is floated out of the house into the woods and then into an alien spacecraft. He is shown a needle and thinks it is put into his brain. Then he feels he is being raped anally. Later, under hypnosis, he recalls more details of the experience. Later still, he has another "missing time" experience and several visits from little "dwarf-like" beings.

Strieber then starts seeing a psychiatrist, Dr. Donald Klein, who uses regressive hypnosis, and after a number of hypnotic sessions concludes, "I have examined Whitley Strieber and found that he is not suffering from a psychosis. He appears to me to have adapted very well to life at a high level of uncertainty. He is not hallucinating in a manner characteristic of psychosis." Dr. Klein also wrote that many of Strieber's symptoms were consistent with temporal lobe abnormality, thus raising the question of possible organic brain disease. Subsequent EEG tests, however, revealed no abnormalities. Strieber also took a lie detector test and this test indicated that he honestly thought he perceived the things reported in the book.

UFO Abductions Demystified

To fully understand the behavior of people reporting having been abducted by aliens in UFOs, we need to review a number of concepts: confabulation, memory creation, inadvertent and advertent cueing, fantasy-prone personalities and psychological needs, hypnogogic and hypnopompic hallucinations, and the missing time experience, and see how they apply to the abduction matter.

Confabulation, or the tendency of ordinary individuals to confuse fact with fiction and under hypnosis to report fantasy events as actual occurrences is well known. Certainly in the case of claimed UFO abductions, many of the stories elicited and solicited by the hypnotist can be expected to contain a large amount of confabulation. Even if the abduction experiences are believed to be "real" by the individuals being regressed, this is no proof that such things actually happened.

An experiment by A.H. Lawson and W.C. McCall (1977) of California State University is relevant here. They hypnotically induced imaginary UFO abductions in a group of subjects, who were then questioned about their experience. Not only were these subjects able to tell plausible stories about what happened to them aboard their imaginary flying saucers, but their stories showed no substantive differences from tales in the UFO literature by persons who claimed to have actually experienced an abduction. In 1978 Lawson read a paper at an American Psychological Association meeting which contained a revised account of the experiment. He pointed out some differences between the findings of the experiment and the tales in the UFO literature, along with the many similarities. He also warned that it was important to be very cautious about using the results from hypnotic regressions, since a witness can lie and even believe his own lies, thus invalidating the investigation.

It is also common knowledge that hypnotized witnesses subtly confuse their own fantasies with reality, without either the witness or the hypnotist being aware of what is happening. Martin Orne has warned again and again of the dangers of using hypnosis as a means of getting at the truth.

Not only do we translate beliefs into memories even when we are wide awake, but in the case of hypnotized witnesses with few specific memories, the hypnotist may unwittingly (or wittingly in some cases) suggest memories and create in the witness a number of crucial and vivid recollections of events that never happened, i.e., pseudomemories.

Guided Suggestibility

A classic example of the effect of suggestion on people who are wide awake is shown by a demonstration carried out by magician and mentalist Kreskin a few years ago in Ottawa. Dr. Alan Hynek, an astronomer, was also present and was interested in the contagion of UFO sightings or guided suggestibility—i.e., one reported UFO sighting is invariably followed by several more, because the suggestion is "contagious." Having set up cameras outside the television studio, in the studio Kreskin "conditioned" fourteen subjects and then told them that after the next commercial they were to go outside, and when he dropped a handkerchief they would see three flying objects. In his words,

> I watched for a moment and then went outdoors to join them, Dr. Hynek following. The night was clear, icy cold. Stars were out. Mingling with them near the reporter, I pulled out the handkerchief, wiped my forehead with it and then dropped it. In a few seconds the fourteen subjects were sighting three flying saucers, pointing up and discussing them with Keeping [the news director]. Skepticism had vanished.

> One man rushed back into the studio, asking permission to use the phone to report UFOs. Studio personnel, briefed on what was occurring refused his request. He returned outside, bitterly denouncing the studio employees for their apathy.

> I then said in a loud voice, that it appeared to me that one of the saucers was descending and that it would probably hover over the station within a few minutes. Two of the subjects began running across the snowy field toward the high-

way. I yelled, "Release," and they turned back; the other twelve subjects responded to the same signal.

Keeping began asking them about the saucers. Uniformly, the subjects either laughed at him or questioned his sanity. No one had seen "flying saucers."

Dr. Hynek was very interested to know exactly what they had seen. We all returned inside, out of subfreezing weather, and I suggested that the fourteen subjects back into their imaginative mental discovery. They responded in considerable detail including descriptions of shapes and designs of the UFOs. The colors varied; some saw yellow saucers and some saw green. Notably, no subject saw more than three saucers, the exact number I had suggested.

Later that night the astronomer (Dr. Hynek) concluded that suggestibility had played a much larger role in UFO sightings, where more than one person was involved, than previously thought. People had hallucinated saucers or huge metal cigars. It was not a distortion of reality but a sighting of "nothing". . . .

In the case of the fourteen subjects in Ottawa, they responded in the heat of the experiment and afterward, but in a comparatively short time they would have realized what had happened, as with all cases of suggestibility. The psychodrama keyed by suggestion is never permanent.

Individuals who continue to report "private" incidents with UFOs, as though selected by that other intelligence as contact person for the "earth planet", have to be suspect. There is no physical evidence to back up their sightings. The attention given to them or the commitment made to themselves on the initial sighting probably forces them on. Nonetheless, they are quite capable of contagion within a group, as is the person who genuinely hallucinates and genuinely believes he has spotted a spaceship from another galaxy. (Kreskin 1973, pp. 125–126)

If individuals are this suggestible without any formal induction per se (certainly, Kreskin's "conditioning" is an effective suggestive tool), we must consider the effects of suggestion when the subjects are invited and encouraged to become imaginatively involved with the hypnotist's script and wishes. It is also important to recognize that deeply hypnotized subjects (i.e., those who are deeply involved in the game), may not only willfully lie but may become expert at doing so. When we also consider that most psychologists and psychiatrists are not particularly skillful at detecting and recognizing deception, and certainly have not been trained to do so, it becomes even harder to determine whether a subject was or was not telling the truth.

Real and Created Memories

Orne also has warned that hypnotic suggestions to relive a past event, particularly when accompanied by questions about specific details, put pressure on the subject to provide information for which few if any actual memories are available. While this situation may stimulate the subject's memory and produce some increased recall, it can also cause him to confabulate. Moreover, there is no way anyone can determine whether such information is from actual memory or is confabulation, unless somehow or other one is able to obtain an independent verification. Even more troubling is the fact that if the hypnotist has beliefs about what happened, it is almost impossible for him to prevent himself from inadvertently steering the subject's recall in such a way that the subject will remember what the hypnotist believes! Elizabeth Loftus also has warned that no one—not even the most sophisticated hypnotist—can tell the difference between a memory that is real and one that has been created (Loftus 1979). If a person who is highly suggestible is hypnotized and false information is implanted in his mind, he tends to believe it. And even polygraphs cannot distinguish between real and phony memory.

As mentioned earlier, inadvertent cueing is also of great

importance in UFO abduction fantasies. By this means the hypnotist unintentionally signals to the person being regressed exactly what response is wanted. Through inadvertent cueing it is even possible to give post-hypnotic suggestions prior to the induction of hypnosis. In some cases it has been found that other people in the same room with the subject and the hypnotist have inadvertently communicated to the subject what they are expecting to happen, i.e., what pleases them, what displeases them, what excites them or bores them, and so on. Ian Wilson (1981), has shown that hypnotically elicited reports of reincarnation vary directly as a function of the hypnotist's beliefs about reincarnation. And Laurence, Nadon, Nogrady and Perry (1986) have shown that pseudomemories were also elicited by inadvertent cueing in the use of hypnosis by police. . . .

Is Hypnosis Dangerous?

The above question might be better phrased: Are relaxation, suggestion, and freeing the individual's imagination dangerous? Or we might as well ask: Is water dangerous? Are automobiles dangerous? Is salt dangerous? Are aspirins dangerous? Is life dangerous? (It certainly is. No one ever gets out of it alive!)

The answer to all of these questions is—well, yes and no. While water is necessary to life, too much of it at the wrong time and place can cause drowning. Just because hundreds of people are killed every year in auto accidents doesn't mean that we will stop using them. Just because if we take too many aspirins at once we will poison ourselves doesn't mean we should ban this painkiller. Just about anything and everything can be dangerous if it is misused or misapplied or amassed in such quantifies that it threatens life and limb.

Of all the things mentioned above, hypnosis is perhaps

the least dangerous. There are no deaths on record due specifically to hypnosis. . . .

Yet for every general rule it seems there is always at least one exception or qualification. The only thing dangerous about hypnosis is its attractiveness for naive or self-seeking individuals like Budd Hopkins and other abduction gurus who convince incipient paranoids and/or the fantasy-prone that their worst fears have been realized and that they were victims of alien monsters who abducted them, invaded their bodies, and are still monitoring their behavior. As Philip Klass (1989) has observed, such alleged UFO abductions are "a dangerous game," and grievous mental harm is being done to many innocent and trusting individuals in need of skilled professional help who instead receive treatment at the hands of fanatics like Hopkins.

References

Fowler, R. 1979. *The Andreasson Affair: The Documented Investigation of a Woman's Abduction Aboard a UFO.* Englewood Cliffs, N.J.: Prentice-Hall.

Fuller, J. 1966. *The Interrupted Journey.* New York: Dial Press.

Hopkins, B. 1987. *Intruders: The Incredible Visitations at Copley Woods.* New York: Random House.

———. 1981. *Missing Time.* New York: G.P. Putnam's Sons.

Keyhoe, D. 1955. *The Flying Saucer Conspiracy.* New York: Holt, Rinehart and Winston.

Klass, P.J. 1989. *UFO Abductions: A Dangerous Game.* Buffalo: Prometheus Books.

Kreskin. 1973. *The Amazing World of Kreskin.* New York: Random House.

Laurence, J.R., Nadon, R., Nogrady, H., and Perry, C. 1986. "Duality, dissociation, and memory creation in highly hypnotizable subjects." *Int. J. Clin. Exp. Hypnosis* 34:295–310.

Lawson, A.H., and McCall, W.C. 1977. "What can we learn from the hypnosis of imaginary abductees?" MUFON UFO Symposium Proceedings, Seguin, Texas; Mutual UFO Network. Pp. 107–135.

Loftus, E. 1979. *Eyewitness Testimony.* Cambridge, Mass.: Harvard University Press.

Orne, M.T. 1979. "The use and misuse of hypnosis in court." *Intl. J. Clin. Exp. Hypnosis* 27:311–341.

Strieber, W. 1987. *Communion: A True Story.* New York: Beach Tree Books, Wm. Morrow Co.

Wilson, I. 1981. *Mind Out of Time.* London: Gollancz Publishers.

Alien Abductees Have Fantasy-Prone Personalities

Robert E. Bartholomew and George S. Howard

A study of alien abductees and contactees showed that while they were not mentally ill, a significant portion of them were identified as having fantasy-prone personality (FPP). The general population is largely free of FPP, which is defined as having a rich fantasy life as adults and being easily hypnotized or having psychic abilities, out-of-body experiences, or religious visions or other apparitions. Robert E. Bartholomew is a researcher in sociology at James Cook University of North Queensland, Australia. George S. Howard is a professor of psychology at the University of Notre Dame. They are the authors of *UFOs and Alien Contact: Two Centuries of Mystery*.

> Whatever these anomalies may or may not be, one thing is
> certain: they keep on happening. They have survived cen-
> turies of misattribution and misunderstanding, of doubt
> and debunking. Prophets and psychics still perform . . .
> prodigies, ordinary men and women continue to report ex-
> traordinary sights and sounds. If this is all an illusion, then
> it is high time that the mechanism of such persistent illu-
> sion was revealed.   —Hilary Evans[1]

Psychopathological interpretations of individuals claiming contacts with extraterrestrials typify the few psychiatric
evaluations of such behavior. This viewpoint will present biographical analysis performed on 154 subjects reporting
temporary abductions or persistent contacts with UFO occupants. The 154 case histories are remarkably devoid of a
history of mental illness. However, in 132 cases, identifica-
tions were made with one and often several major characteristics of what psychologists S.C. Wilson and T. X. Barber[2]
first identified as the fantasy-prone personality (FPP), a set
of characteristics not typically found in the general population. While functioning as normal, healthy adults, FPPs experience rich fantasy lives, scoring dramatically higher (rel-
ative to control groups) on such characteristics as hypnotic
susceptibility, psychic ability, healing, out-of-body experiences, automatic writing, religious visions, and apparitional
experiences. In our study, UFO "abductees" and "contactees" evidence a similar pattern of characteristics to FPPs.

Are You Crazy?

Imagine you have a new neighbor whom you meet for the
first time. The neighbor calmly describes the following
event: "I know you'll find this hard to believe, but last week
I was abducted by aliens who held me for about seven hours
in their spaceship." After careful questioning, you find that
your new neighbor believes that he is also telepathic, has

had religious visions in the past, and spent a large part of his childhood conversing with an imaginary playmate. You describe the neighbor to a friend, who asks, "Is there extreme psychopathology here? Do you believe your neighbor is severely disturbed?" What would be your answer?

Ever since mass sightings of flying saucers were first reported, those claiming contact with saucer occupants (or even some claiming to watch such craft at a distance) were often labeled socially deviant or mentally disturbed. Such diagnoses were often based on the fantastic nature of the claims and not on firsthand psychological evaluation. Despite the unreliability of eyewitness testimony[3] and the ambiguous nature of most flying saucer reports (usually misinterpretations of ordinary celestial objects[4]), the media has typically attributed sightings to "psychopathological disturbances in the witness."[5]

While there are few psychological studies of people claiming regular communication with extraterrestrials—contactees—or temporary abductions aboard a spaceship—abductees—virtually all such people have been characterized as mentally disturbed or irrational. Psychologists Lester Grinspoon and Alan D. Persky,[6] for instance, explain many contact claims as psychopathological, the result of *folie á deux* psychosis and psychopathic personalities, yet these authors failed to study witnesses firsthand or cite a single case. Of six patients claiming contacts with extraterrestrials, psychiatrists L. Mavrakis and J. Bocquet[7] diagnosed five as suffering from a paranoid delusional state. In applying a psychoanalytic perspective to members of the "flying saucer subculture," John A. Keel[8] classifies many contactees as "neurotic and paranoid personalities" (p. 871). Both Carl Jung and Joost Meerloo[9] relate the phenomena to the need for the existence of a higher power and the likelihood that many experiences result from repressed, infantile sexually orientated conflicts. Similar interpretations have been made by sociologists who characterize typical members of flying-saucer clubs, particularly those reporting contacts, as mentally ill:

> [In] flying saucer clubs I have had contact with . . . by any conventional definition the mental health . . . is quite low. Hallucinations are quite common. . . . If one were to attend a meeting and watch the action without knowing in advance whether the audience was in a mental hospital or not, it would be very difficult to tell, because many symptoms of serious illness are displayed.[10]

This psychopathological interpretation is not unlike the labels ascribed to people accused of witchcraft during the sixteenth and seventeenth centuries. "Witches" were considered "maniacs or melancholics," "detracted in mind,"[11] or suffering from disorders of "neuropathology," as was believed by Charcot, Esquirol, Janet, and Freud.[12] This classification has held until recent times, with the work of Zilboorg,[13] that most medieval witches were considered mentally ill. The predominant interpretation of witchcraft during the past twenty years, however, has shifted. The contemporary view is predicated on detailed historical and archival research and has shifted toward a culturally relativistic position considering the unique historical sociocultural milieu of individuals and their behavior.[14]

Boston-area psychiatrist Dr. Benjamin Simon's use of hypnotherapy with a couple claiming a UFO abduction,[15] Florida psychiatrist Dr. Bertold Schwarz's in-depth evaluations of abduction and contact victims who were found to be mentally healthy,[16] and Mavrakis and Bocquet's[17] examination of contact and abduction subjects are the only firsthand psychological studies of UFO abductees and contactees known to exist. While such firsthand evaluations are beyond the scope of the present study, we will compare the characteristics of a sample of UFO abductees and contactees from archival data with the "fantasy-prone personality"[18] (FPP). On the basis of this comparison, suggestions for the psychological understanding of such cases will be discussed.

The Fantasy-Prone Personality

There is an entire class of normal, healthy individuals who are prone to experiencing exceptionally vivid and involved fantasies. Such people often have difficulty distinguishing between fantasy and reality and tend to keep their fantasy worlds closely guarded secrets. Based on preliminary research by J. R. Hilgard[19] and subsequent work by Wilson and Barber,[20] approximately 4 percent of the population falls into the FPP category, ranging in degree from mild to intense. Wilson and Barber uncovered this category while administering a battery of tests and interviews to twenty-seven "excellent" and twenty-five "nonexcellent" female hypnotic subjects.[21] Their findings have since received support in studies using more heterogeneous samples.[22] The results of these investigations have implications for understanding an important component in many UFO abduction and contact reports, especially those who persistently report such phenomena and who have typically been considered to be psychopathological.

In providing a brief overview of their findings, Wilson and Barber noted that most fantasy-prone subjects (92 percent) estimated spending half or more of their working day fantasizing, compared to 0 percent in their control group.[23] In discussing the vividness of their subjects' experiences, Wilson and Barber found that the fantasy-prone actually "see," "hear," "smell," and "feel" what is being described in conversations or on television.[24] Sixty-five percent of the FPPs reported that their fantasies were "as real as real" (hallucinatory) in all sense modalities and were experienced in an "automatic" or "involuntary" manner (compared to 0 percent in the control group).

> They see sights equally well with their eyes opened or closed. Also, imagined aromas are sensed, imagined sounds are heard, and imagined tactile sensations are felt as convincingly as those produced by actual stimuli. . . . Almost all of the fantasy-prone subjects have vivid sexual fantasies that they experience "as real as real" with all the sights, sounds, smells, emotions, feelings, and physical sensations . . . [and they] are so realistic that 75 percent of the fantasizers report that they have had orgasms produced solely by sexual fantasies.[25]

Fifty-eight percent of the FPPs (8 percent in the control group) reported spending a "large part" of their childhood playing or interacting with fantasized people or animals (so-called imaginary friends), claiming to have "clearly seen, heard and felt them in the same way that they perceived living people and animals."[26]

As children, all but one of the FPPs lived in a make-believe world much or most of the time. Of those playing with dolls or toy animals, 80 percent believed them to be living, with unique feelings and personalities. While imaginary playmates are common in children, and in recent years have been viewed as a sign of mental health and creativity,[27] there are important differences between the fantasy-prone and control groups on this dimension.

> Many of the twenty-five subjects in the comparison group also pretended their dolls or stuffed animals were alive; however, with three exceptions, they did so only when they were playing with them. Although they made-believe that the dolls and toy animals had personalities and said and did specific things, the make-believe play was always confined to a specific period and the toys did not seem to have an independent life.[28]

While most (perhaps all) children play make-believe games, it is uncommon for them to continue with imaginary companions into adulthood. But the extensiveness and vividness of imaginary companions apparently does not decrease substantially for the fantasy-prone group as adults. Based on their findings, Wilson and Barber hypothesized that many figures from history who claimed psychic or paranormal experiences may have been fantasy-prone.[29]. . .

UFOs and "Psychic" Phenomena: Results

Wilson and Barber have noted a significant relationship between subjects reporting frequent "psychic" occurrences and FPPs. For example, while 92 percent of the FPPs they studied see themselves as psychic or sensitive and report numerous telepathic and precognitive experiences, just 16 percent of the comparison group reported such experiences.[30] In the present sample, 75 percent were categorized as psychic and/or telepathic or experiencing poltergeist activity. It seems plausible that psychic incidents may have been perceived by a greater number of subjects but were unreported in the biographies, as most of the subjects' accounts typically center on the UFO experience, not their psychic history.

Out-of-Body Experiences

Of Wilson and Barber's fantasy group 88 percent (compared to 8 percent of comparison group subjects) reported "realistic out-of-the-body experiences."[31] By comparison, in our sample 21 percent reported "astral travel," "astral projection," "out-of-body experiences," "bi-location," or body floating. Again, because of the differences in data collection procedures employed with our sample of subjects, this 21 percent estimate could well be a serious underestimate. These experiences typically occur about equally with lone subjects or within a séance with multiple witnesses. During the 1860s, William Denton of Massachusetts was a popular spirit medium and lecturer who claimed to astrally project his body, enabling him to contact beings from Venus and describe to onlookers the content of his experiences.[32] . . .

The Contemporary Social Context

The current social milieu plays a role in the relationship between the fantasy-prone process and the FPPs' worldview. The FPPs living in the twentieth century are heavily exposed to books, television programs, and movies on the subject of extraterrestrial visitation. It is only natural, therefore, to expect their experiences to reflect the science-fiction and popular beliefs of the time. This could explain why prior to the nineteenth century there are virtually no explicit reported contacts with extraterrestrials. Yet, in the United Kingdom and Europe especially, there were thousands of reported sightings, abductions, and contacts with fairies at this time.[33] This relationship between UFO encounters and fairy lore was first mentioned by British investigator Gordon Creighton and later by French astrophysicist Dr. Jacques Vallee, Loren Coleman, Jerome Clark, John Rimmer, and Hilary Evans.[34]

Our preliminary findings suggest that the similarities between characteristics of FPPs and UFO abductees and contactees is a potentially fruitful avenue of research. While not all UFO abductees and contactees are FPPs, this exploratory study supports the hypothesis that a significant portion of this population falls into the FPP category. Unfortunately, FPPs experiencing UFO-related contacts and abductions may have often been labeled as psychopathological. In this regard, it is appropriate to quote from Wilson and Barber, who hint at the potential for significant others or therapists to enrich the lives of FPPs by helping them understand their syndrome.

> Most of those we saw again later told us that our interviews had made a significant difference in their lives. They typi-

cally stated that they had gained greater understanding of themselves and felt less alone—previously they had assumed that no one else was like them. Following participation in our project, some of the fantasizers felt ready to share their "secret" with important people in their lives. One told her husband of twenty years and gave him a copy of our preliminary report of the study[35] so that he could see her as she really was. Another gave a copy . . . to her counselor so that he could understand her.[36]

Finally, it is interesting to note the shifting content of contemporary FPPs. If abductees and contactees are over-represented as fantasy-prone personalities, instead of romantic visions of fairies of yesteryear, the images of the modern-day FPP reflect the period and culture into which they are born. It is not surprising, then, that the earliest, most common alien messages concerned fear of nuclear destruction. Recently, the messages have warned of the approaching ecological problems that face our planet.

[A]bduction reports are important. They contain a message about ourselves . . . a message put forward by a growing number of people who have perhaps no other way of expressing the anxieties and crises of their lives. . . . It is a message given to us by the hidden parts of our being, and it is a message we should listen to carefully.[37]

We are all frightened by the possibilities of a catastrophic future for our world. If humans are to take effective actions to forestall such horrors, someone must first identify the horrific possibilities. Our problem is that articulating anticipated catastrophes is a difficult task for many people. Perhaps having God speak through a prophet or an alien speak through an abductee represents a psychologically easier way to address future nuclear or ecological horrors. The messages of modern UFO abductees and contactees mirror the anxieties prevalent in the societies of their times.

Notes

1. H. Evans, *Intrusions—Society and the Paranormal* (London: Routledge and Kegan Paul, 1982).

2. S.C. Wilson and T.X. Barber, "Vivid Fantasy and Hallucinatory Abilities in the Life Histories of Excellent Hypnotic Subjects ('Somnambules'): Preliminary Report with Female Subjects," in E. Klinger, ed., *Imagery, Volume 2, Concepts, Results, and Applications* (New York: Plenum Press, 1981).

3. R. Buckhout, "Eyewitness Testimony," *Scientific American* 231 (1974): 23–31; E.F. Loftus and J.C. Palmer, "Reconstruction of Automobile Destruction: An Example of the Interaction Between Language and Memory," *Journal of Verbal Learning and Verbal Behavior* 13 (1974): 585–89; G. Wells and J. Turtle, "Eyewitness Identification: The Importance of Lineup Models," *Psychological Bulletin* 99 (1968): 320–29.

4. J.A.M. Meerloo, "Le Syndrome des Soucoupes Volantes," *Medecine et Hygiene* 25 (1967): 992–96.

5. B. Schwarz, "Psychiatric and Parapsychiatric Dimensions of UFOs," in R. Haines, ed., *UFO Phenomena and the Behavioral Scientist* (Metuchen, N.J.: Scarecrow Press, 1979).

6. L. Grinspoon and A.D. Persky, "Psychiatry and UFO Reports," in C. Sagan and T. Page, eds., *UFOs: A Scientific Debate* (Ithaca, N.Y.: Cornell University Press, 1973).

7. D. Mavrakis and J. Bocquet, "Psychoses et Objets Volants Non Identifies" [Psychoses and unidentified flying objects], *Canadian Journal of Psychiatry* 28 (1983): 199–201.

8. J.A. Keel, "The Flying Saucer Subculture," *Journal of Popular Culture* 5 (1975): 871–96.

9. C.G. Jung, *Flying Saucers: A Modern Myth of Things Seen in the Sky*, trans. R.F.C. Hull (New York: Harcourt, Brace and World, 1959); Meerloo, "Le Syndrome"; J.A.M. Meerloo, "The Flying Saucer Syndrome and the Need for Miracles," *Journal of the American Medical Association* 203 (1968): 170.

10. H.T. Buckner, "The Flying Saucerians: An Open Door Cult," in M. Truzzi, ed., *Sociology in Everyday Life* (Englewood Cliffs, N.J.: Prentice-Hall, 1968).

11. W.E.H. Lecky, *History of European Morals Volumes I and II* (reprint, New York: Braziller, 1955).

12. T.S. Szasz, *The Manufacture of Madness* (New York: Harper &

Row, 1970); T.J. Schoeneman, "Criticisms of the Psycho-pathological Interpretation of Witch Hunts: A Review," *American Journal of Psychiatry* 139 (1982): 1028–32.

13. G.A. Zilboorg, *The Medical Man and the Witch during the Renaissance*. The Hideyo Nogushi Lecures (Baltimore: Johns Hopkins Press, 1935); G.A. Zilboorg and G.W. Henry, *History of Medical Psychology* (New York: W. W. Norton, 1941).

14. G. Rosen, *Madness in Society: Chapters in the Historical Sociology of Mental Illness* (New York: Harper & Row, 1968); Szasz, *Manufacture of Madness*; J. Kroll, "A Reappraisal of Psychiatry in the Middle Ages," *Archives of General Psychiatry* 29 (1973): 276–83; N. P. Spanos, "Witchcraft in Histories of Psychiatry: A Critical Analysis and an Alternative Conceptualization," *Psychological Bulletin* 85 (1978): 417–39; R. Neugebauer, "Treatment of the Mentally Ill in Medieval and Early Modern England: A Reappraisal," *Journal of the History of the Behavioral Sciences* 14 (1978): 158–69; Schoeneman, "Criticisms of Psychopathological Interpretation."

15. B. Simon, "Hypnosis in the Treatment of Military Neuroses," *Psychiatric Opinion* 4 (1967): 24–29.

16. B.E. Schwarz, "UFOs: Delusion or Dilemma?" *Medical Times* 96 (1968): 967–81; B. E. Schwarz, "UFOs in New Jersey," *Journal of the Medical Society of New Jersey* 68 (1969): 460–64. B.E. Schwarz, "UFO Contactee Stella Lansing: Possible Medical Implications of Her Motion Picture Experiments," paper presented at 1975 annual meeting of the American Society of Psychosomatic Dentistry and Medicine, Montclair, N.J., September 21, 1975. This paper was published the next year in *Journal of the American Society of Psychosomatic Dentistry and the American Society of Psychosomatic Denistry and Medicine* 23 (1976): 60–68; B. E. Schwarz, *UFO Dynamics: Book I* (Florida: Rainbow, 1983a); B. E. Schwarz, *UFO Dynamics: Book II* (Florida: Rainbow, 1983b).

17. Mavrakis and Bocquet, "Psychoses et Objets Volants Non Identifies."

18. Wilson and Barber, "Vivid Fantasy and Hallucinatory Abilities."

19. J.R. Hilgard, *Personality and Hypnosis: A Study of Imaginative Involvement* (Chicago: University of Chicago Press, 1970); J.R. Hilgard, *Personality and Hypnosis: A Study of Imaginative Involvement*, 2d ed. (Chicago: University of Chicago Press, 1979).

20. Wilson and Barber, "Vivid Fantasy and Hallucinatory Abilities"; S.C. Wilson and T.X. Barber, "The Fantasy-Prone Personality: For Understanding Imagery, Hypnosis, and Parapsychological Phenomena," in A.A. Sheikh, ed., *Imagery: Current Theory, Research, and Application* (New York: Wiley, 1983).

21. Wilson and Barber, "Fantasy-Prone Personality."

22. S. Myers and H. Austrin, "Distal Eidetic Technology: Further Characteristics of the Fantasy-Prone Personality," *Journal of Mental Imagery* 9 (1985): 7–66; S. Lynn and J. Rhue, "The Fantasy-Prone Person: Hypnosis, Imagination, and Creativity," *Journal of Personality and Social Psychology* 51 (1986): 404–408; S. Lynn and J. Rhue, "Fantasy-Proneness and Psychopathology," *Personality and Social Psychology* 53 (1987): 327–36; S. Lynn and J. Rhue, "Fantasy Proneness: Developmental Antecedents," *Journal of Personality* 55 (1987): 1.

23. Wilson and Barber, "Fantasy-Prone Personality."

24. Ibid.

25. Ibid., p. 351.

26. Ibid., p. 346.

27. M. Pines, "Invisible Playmates," *Psychology Today* 12 (1978): 38–42.

28. Wilson and Barber, "Fantasy-Prone Personality," p. 346.

29. Ibid.

30. Ibid.

31. Ibid.

32. W. Denton, *The Soul of Things* (Boston: privately published, 1873); J. Hudson, *Those Sexy Saucer People* (San Diego: Greenleaf Classics, 1967); Keel, "Flying Saucer Subculture," pp. 871–96. Of lone percipients reporting astral experiences, a quiet setting, such as meditation or resting in bed prior to sleep, appears to induce the experience. Contactee William Ferguson always began his numerous encounters during meditation. His experiences were consciousness-raising, providing keen insights into his life.

> Upon my return to Earth . . . I thought I would go into the living room where an old gentleman . . . was staying at my house . . . to see if he would recognize me. As I went into the living room I spoke to him, but there was

no response. He couldn't see nor hear me. . . . There were a lot of things I could do and think about and understand, that I never could have understood before. So I went back to the room where I had been relaxing, . . . and I looked for my body, but my body isn't there, . . . I again placed myself upon the lounge and remained quiet until my being was transformed back into this three-dimensional dense matter projection, and thereupon went into the dining room and told my wife about my experience. (W. Ferguson, *My Trip to Mars* [Potomac, Md.: Cosmic Study Center, 1954]).

33. R. Kirk, *The Secret Commonwealth of Elves, Fauns and Fairies* (London: Longman, 1815); T. Keightley, *The Fairy Mythology* (England, n.p., 1815); W.Y. Evans-Wentz, *The Fairy-Faith in Celtic Countries* (Rennes, France, 1909); K. Briggs, *An Encyclopedia of Fairies* (New York: Pantheon, 1976).

34. G. Creighton, "Postscript to the Most Amazing Case of All," *Flying Saucer Review* 11 (1965): pp. 24–25; J. Vallee, *Passport to Magonia—From Folklore to Flying Saucers* (Chicago: Henry Regnery, 1969); L. Coleman and J. Clark, *The Unidentified* (New York: Warner, 1975); J. Rimmer, *The Evidence for Alien Abductions* (Wellingborough, Northamptonshire: Aquarian, 1984); H. Evans, *The Evidence for UFOs* (Wellingborough: Aquarian, 1983); H. Evans, *Visions, Apparitions, Alien Visitors* (Wellingborough: Aquarian, 1984).

35. Wilson and Barber, "Vivid Fantasy and Hallucinatory Abilities."

36. Wilson and Barber, "Fantasy-Prone Personality," p. 367.

37. Rimmer, *Evidence for Alien Abductions*, p. 153.

The Burden of Proof Does Not Support Claims of Alien Visitation

Jim Giglio and Scott Snell

There is no scientific evidence that aliens have visited the Earth. The laws of physics dictate that no object can travel faster than the speed of light; in addition, a spacecraft traveling faster than the speed of sound must create a sonic boom, a phenomenon that has never been mentioned when people report a UFO sighting. The evidence in support of alien visitation consists entirely of statements by people who claim to have observed unusual phenomena. This evidence cannot be given more weight than sound scientific principles that have stood the test of time for hundreds of years. Jim Giglio and Scott Snell are board members of the National Capital Area Skeptics, an organization based in the Washington, D.C., area that promotes critical thinking.

Let's start where any scientific debate over the UFO evidence ought to start, with the 1968 University of Colorado report to the Air Force. That project examined the evidence that had accumulated since 1947; it was, and remains, the largest scientific study ever conducted in relation to the UFO issue. The principal conclusion was narrowly focused and stated with considerable precision:

> Careful consideration of the record as it is available to us leads us to conclude that further extensive study of UFOs probably cannot be justified in the expectation that science will be advanced thereby.

It should be noted that the report did not state that the hypothesis of extraterrestrial visitation had been conclusively disproved, only that the evidence accumulated up to that time in relation to the issue had contributed nothing to science and showed no sign of contributing anything in the future.

Standing the Test of Time

How well has that conclusion stood the test of time?

Examine the sighting report that Richard Dolan regards as typical and informative. The report was submitted to the National UFO Reporting Center in 1999 and refers to an event that allegedly occurred in 1976 near Hydes, Maryland:

> it was dusk that day. we saw this round craft come out of the northeast over the horizon. it was slowly rotating counter clockwise. white lights only, were on the outer edges. it moved slowly, maybe 30 to 40 miles per hour. it came directly over us. we were on a horse farm, laying on the front lawn just after dinner. this craft was just below the sunlight that was left in the sky. we could not see any details. when it came over us, it stopped. then separated into four smaller

craft. then at the blink of an eye, they shot over the horizon. each ship went directly north, south, east and west respectively. there was absolutely no sound from this craft. we learned the next day that there were sightings over peach-bottom atomic plant that day. the same direction that our craft came from. to this day, we have never spoken about this to anyone, not even between ourselves. there were 6 of us. two music teachers, a medical lab tech, a texas instruments tech, police officer, a kindergarten teacher.

As scientific evidence, this statement has numerous "red flags" hanging all over it. The writer, supposedly a professional, seems not to want to bother with the standard capitalization rules for English sentences. The statement is only semi-coherent, with sentences describing various aspects of the incident tumbling over each other in a rush; with 23 years to think about the incident, it ought to have been possible to organize the description into a coherent narrative. (S)he reports that no details of the object could be seen, yet states that it was 1000 feet in diameter and traveling 30 or 40 miles per hour. How these size and speed determinations were made is unspecified, nor is there an explanation for an inability to resolve details when it *was* possible to determine size and speed. Accepting the size and speed estimates leads to another problem. Hydes, Maryland, is located near a number of heavily-traveled highways and air transportation corridors. Near-by observers should have numbered in the thousands and generated numerous newspaper headlines; we are referred, instead, to some alleged sightings at a nuclear power plant located a considerable distance away.

Typical, but Worthless

Mr. Dolan informs us that this kind of report is typical. He's quite right; it *is* typical, but as scientific evidence it's worthless. Individuals and organizations adhering to the notion of ET visitation accumulate reports like this by the thousands and periodically present them to the public to support their position. There's a logical fallacy at work in this constant piling-up of reports, the fallacy that large amounts of bad evidence somehow add up to good evidence. They don't. You can't make a silk purse out of a sow's ear, nor can you make one out of 10,000 sow's ears. The Colorado investigators were right; despite their volume, reports such as this, which had contributed nothing to science as of 1968, have yet to contribute anything in the intervening 33 years.

The fact that Mr. Dolan gives credence to this flawed statement illustrates an aspect of the UFO issue that ought to trouble proponents of the notion that this issue is a serious scientific problem. We refer to an apparent unwillingness, on the part of far too many of these proponents, to apply even a modicum of critical thinking to such reports.

One of us (Scott) recently attended a UFO conference. At this event, a physicist widely considered to be a technically adept investigator (who shall remain nameless) gave a presentation in which he described his analysis of photos showing peculiar lights over the night skyline of an Arizona city. He showed the audience how he had compared the lights of the city in the two different photos that the witness claimed had been taken only a few moments apart. There was no question that the city lights had changed markedly. Test photos taken for comparison showed that one was taken sometime before 11 P.M. and the other taken sometime afterwards, despite the witness's claim that both were taken in quick succession at about 8 P.M. (At about 11 P.M., skyline lighting changes significantly as businesses and homes turn off their lights for the night.) The investigator then asked the witness for the photographic negatives. He learned that the two photos were actually from *different rolls of film*, separated by several other frames, some showing only the skyline, some showing only the peculiar "UFO" lights (This aspect of the report is striking in its resemblance to the Colorado report's Case #7.)

At this point, a listener to the talk might have expected the investigator to conclude that this was not a reliable case to proceed with. The witness's story did not jibe with the photographic facts, and the contents of the interim photos suggested experiments in trick photography. But the listener would have been wrong. The investigator touted this as "missing time discovered through photo analysis." (For the uninitiated, the "missing time" phenomenon is a standard component of alien abduction stories; it occurs when someone notices that the time on a clock or watch is considerably later than expected; the abduction event that supposedly occupied this time is somehow erased from memory.)

When questioned as to his conclusions, the investigator stressed that " . . . the witness is a very credible, respected member of her community. She would not have lied about it." Apparently this investigator had never read Colorado case 7; that hoaxer was a retired military officer with an "irreproachable" reputation. The investigator also apparently never heard of Occam's Razor, the principle which states that, other factors being equal, one chooses the simpler of two competing explanations for an observation.

A High Level of Critical Thinking Is Needed

When one is investigating a UFO incident in the expectation that it might provide evidence that our planet is being visited by ET's (a most extraordinary hypothesis), a high level of critical thinking should be strenuously applied. But in the two examples of "pro-UFO" evidence seen here, this does not appear to be happening. Mr. Dolan supports the flawed statement quoted above, and the audience at the conference was generally accepting of this perfectly ludicrous photo analysis. Acceptance and support of this kind of thing by adherents of the "pro" viewpoint, as if it were serious science, leads the skeptic to wonder, "If this is the good, credible evidence, what does the bad, non-credible stuff look like?"

Actually the two kinds look very similar, because the UFO issue can no longer (post–Colorado report) make a strong claim to being a scientific issue at all. It shows, instead, numerous signs of being a social phenomenon, driven by the print and electronic media, and there is strong evidence that this has been the case all along.

Go back to the beginning, to the Kenneth Arnold sighting. The phenomenon described by Arnold was a group of boomerang-shaped objects that moved like saucers skimming across a water surface. But the report was garbled in initial press reports, leading readers to believe that the alleged objects were saucer-shaped. Subsequent reports, amplified by cinema and television, spread the "saucer" or "disc" image of UFOs to people all over the world. And while many different shapes have been reported for UFOs over the years, the majority of reports have been of saucers or discs, a clear indication that witnesses are seeing what they expect to see, and reporting what others accept as the norm.

The Influence of Television

There is also compelling evidence that the appearance of UFO occupants, as widely accepted among "contact" adherents, arose out of a particular episode of a television series. Barney Hill, who was allegedly abducted by beings from a UFO in the early 1960s (the initial case of this type), went into therapy and was hypnotized in the course of his treatment. Under hypnosis, Hill described the eyes of his abductors as "speaking." This peculiar phrase had been used by an extraterrestrial character in an episode of the ABC-TV series *The Outer Limits*, which had aired only days before Hill's hypnosis session. The episode was "The Bellero Shield;" the alien portrayed was bald, essentially featureless in face and body, and had swept-back eyes, just as Hill sketched under hypnosis. Although other early reports of UFO occupants varied significantly from Hill's (probably inspired by other stereotypical alien images), his description is the one that has saturated popular culture via the media.

In 1975, NBC-TV broadcast a dramatization of Hill's experience in a made-for-TV film called *The UFO Incident*. Many millions of people watched this allegedly true story and learned what aliens are supposed to look like. A couple of years later, Steven Spielberg's *Close Encounters of the Third Kind* became one of the most popular motion pictures ever made, depicting beings similar to those in Hill's description. Public perception of the "standard model" alien was further influenced by the cover of the 1987 best-selling book *Communion*, an allegedly true account of alien contact, which sported the expected image. Had Barney Hill's hypnosis session taken place earlier, or had the ABC network scheduled "The Bellero Shield" later, we would in all likelihood have a different "standard model" alien.

Defying Physics

Let's go on to another kind of evidence, one that is piling up into a rather convincing accumulation. That's the evidence relating to the impossibility of reported UFO behavior under limitations imposed on us by a number of well-tested physical principles. The scientific consensus on these limitations has become more solid over time, making the notion that our planet is being visited by ET spacecraft less and less convincing. (We're assuming here that our hypothetical ET's are conceptualized as physical beings traveling in physical machines from place to place in the here-and-now universe that we see around us. Concepts of "light beings," "interdimensional portals," or "higher vibratory planes" we relegate to the realm of the pseudomystical.)

Crudely stated, the limitations that concern us are:

1. No object travels faster than light (the Einstein speed limit).
2. No object can be made to move without forcing some other object to move in the opposite direction (Newton's 3rd law of motion).
3. No object can move through the atmosphere at bullet-like speeds without creating a sonic boom (a direct consequence of the Doppler effect).
4. Gravity pulls; it can't be made to push.
5. Complex living beings don't survive instantaneous accelerations from a standing start to thousands of miles per hour, nor do they survive instantaneous sharp turns at those speeds (direct consequences of inertia).

Referring to limitation #1, there can be little doubt that if ET's are visiting our planet, they would have to do so in vessels traveling faster than light; sub-light "generation ships" would in all likelihood be totally impractical (more on that idea below). But the Einstein speed limit says this can't be done, so we have to ask: How well-settled is the idea that nothing travels faster than light? Very well indeed, actually, and getting better established all the time. Back in 1947 when the UFO issue first came to prominence, relativity and Dr. Einstein's speed limit were only about 50 years old, and only a handful of experiments had been performed to test their validity. Since then, we've educated several new generations of physicists, many of whom have worked at "pushing the envelope" of relativity. Experiments and theoretical studies have proliferated over this time, but unfortunately no exception has been found to this fundamental limiting principle of physics. In fact, there's not even a realistic hint pointing to the possibility of an exception.

A counter to this argument is the claim that maybe we don't know all the physics there is to know. Of course we don't. But we *do* know a lot, and for almost a century now the evidence has been accumulating that the Einstein speed limit is both intractable and permanent. Anyone who holds that the limit might be bypassed by some "new physics" at some time in the future, or that ET's may already have developed that physics, has a very heavy and rapidly growing burden of proof to bear; solid and convincing evidence, not speculation, is required to support that burden.

Other Limitations

Moving on to the other limitations, it should be noted that these all apply to the standard kinds of behaviors reported for UFOs in the atmosphere. These behaviors include:

1. Instantaneous or near-instantaneous accelerations and decelerations between a dead stop and hypersonic speeds,
2. Instantaneous turns at those hypersonic speeds,
3. Absence of the expected sonic booms from these maneuvers, and
4. Absence of the expected visible indicators of a superpowerful propulsion system at work (smoke, noise, exhaust blast, etc.).

If we assume that some kind of "mothership" brought these craft here across the gulfs of space, and that this mothership complies with the Einstein speed limit (requiring decades or centuries to make the journey), this assumption avoids limitation #1. Unfortunately it won't avoid the other four. To do that, we need such "Star Trek" notions as impulse drive, inertial damping, or anti-gravity. And these are contradicted by ideas that are, if anything, even better-established than the Einstein speed limit, as they are rooted in nearly 400 years of classical physics.

Weighing the Evidence

What we have, then, is a situation where the "pro" evidence consists almost entirely of statements from witnesses who have observed unusual phenomena in the sky and cannot identify what they saw, and whose perceptions and interpretations have been contaminated by images from the popular culture, while the "con" evidence (or at least the strongest such evidence) is a body of physical laws supported by massive amounts of experimental data.

Concerning the "pro" evidence, we know from numerous investigations of those witness accounts that a substantial majority of them (or practically all, depending on your source of information) are explainable as a mix of mundane phenomena observed under odd circumstances, plus a number of hoaxes. As noted above, the Colorado report is enlightening on these points. Taking the case studies as a whole, it is difficult to escape the conclusion that a witness observing something unusual, even a "trained observer," has a near-zero ability to interpret that observation correctly and describe it accurately. It is also difficult to escape the conclusion that reliable individuals, pillars of the community with solid reputations for integrity, pull off UFO hoaxes with surprising frequency.

Concerning the "con" evidence, it needs to be emphasized that the various physical principles in question are approximately 100 to 400 years old, supported by enormous numbers of repeatable experiments and instrumented observations, all subjected to intense scrutiny by generations of scientific professionals who would like nothing better than to demolish an important pillar of the scientific edifice. And these ideas are not just textbook material. Our real-world technology abounds with applications of these ideas, all developed by engineers and inventors who must cope on a daily basis with the inconvenient limitations imposed on them by the physical world and its laws. Aeronautical engineers would be delighted if they could make gravity push rather than pull; inconveniences such as wings and fuel-guzzling engines on airplanes could be dispensed with. The designers of communications equipment and computers would be equally delighted to learn that Dr. Einstein's speed limit could be violated; the possibilities would be dazzling. But alas, none of this is happening, and as the evidence accumulates it appears more likely than ever that it cannot happen, on this planet or any other.

In closing, a final point: The arguments made here are not conclusive. We cannot say with certainty that our planet is not being visited. We can, however, note that those who support the idea of ET visitation have always had a heavy burden of proof, a burden that has only grown heavier as time has passed. We skeptics, who find this idea implausible, have a lighter burden, and it gets lighter with time.

Millions of Americans, and perhaps even tens or hundreds of millions of people worldwide, claim they have been abducted by aliens from another planet. By analyzing the evidence—author credentials, eyewitness testimony, and verifiable facts—offered by the authors in this anthology, readers can perhaps make their own determinations about whether these abduction stories are true or whether the so-called abductees are exaggerating or imagining their experiences.

Alien abduction cannot be studied scientifically because most alleged abductions are unexpected and scientists are rarely around to study and test the phenomenon as it occurs. So ufologists (those who study UFOs and alien abductions) must rely on the personal accounts of people who claim to have been abducted by aliens. Ufologists must take several factors into account when they study abduction reports: whether the eyewitness is reliable; whether any physical evidence exists of an abduction—at the scene or on the abductee's body; and whether there is an alternative explanation for the person's experience.

The Author

In this anthology, two authors prominent in their fields discuss claims of encountering aliens. Bill Chalker, an Australian chemist and ufologist, describes an experience Kary Mullis wrote about in his autobiography. Mullis is a noted chemist who won the Nobel Prize in 1993 for one of his discoveries in chemistry. The fact that Mullis is a Nobel

Prize winner tilts the balance in his favor toward believing his account of alien abduction, as the Nobel Prize is a prestigious award that is given to scientists and researchers who have made important advances in their fields. Although Chalker and Mullis do not specifically say that Mullis was abducted by aliens, they lead readers to that conclusion by recounting an experience that contains many of the classic signs of an alien abduction: seeing an animal with large eyes, such as a raccoon or owl; experiencing "missing time," in which hours have passed without notice, and "waking up" in a different spot than where he should have been; and a sense of recognition when he encounters a story about someone else's alien abduction.

According to Chalker, Mullis maintains he was not under the influence of any drug when he met the glowing raccoon in the woods. After he greeted the raccoon, Mullis asserts that he does not remember anything else from that moment on until early the next morning, when he found himself walking along a road without his flashlight, in dry clothes (when they should have been wet from dew if he had been out all night), and without knowing how he got on the road. When Mullis saw the book *Communion*, a personal account of alien abduction by horror writer Whitley Strieber, he felt an instant sense of recognition. Chalker notes that Mullis concludes his firsthand account very persuasively by arguing that even though he cannot prove through scientific experiments that he met a glowing raccoon, he knows that this experience happened to him.

Michael Shermer is also a believable author. He is the director of the Skeptics Society and the author of several books about skepticism. He recounts being abducted by aliens while participating in a long bicycle race; these aliens, Shermer recalls, looked and acted just like his race support crew. He was convinced the aliens were going to kill him when they tried to get him to sleep in his motorhome. After he awoke from a short nap, he realized that his experience with the "aliens" was a hallucination due to stress and too little sleep. Nevertheless, his "abduction" hallucination remains a vivid memory for him.

Although Shermer is quick to point out that he is not claiming that all other stories of alien abduction are due to stress or sleep deprivation, he does believe that these factors could play a role in many accounts. In fact, Shermer contends that the most logical explanation is also the most likely explanation for unusual occurrences. It is much more likely, he asserts, that a person experienced a hallucination rather than an abduction by aliens.

Hypothetical Reasoning

Readers can use hypothetical reasoning to evaluate whether Chalker/Mullis and Shermer have presented sufficient evidence to support their claims regarding alien abduction. Hypothetical reasoning uses five steps to analyze the evidence:

1. State the author's claim (the hypothesis).
2. Gather the author's evidence supporting the claim.
3. Examine the evidence used to support the claim.
4. Consider alternative explanations that could explain the event.
5. Draw a conclusion about the author's claim.

Hypothetical reasoning can be applied to the articles about alien abduction by Chalker and Shermer to determine which author makes the strongest case. However, reading just two articles probably will not provide enough evidence to determine whether alien abduction is a real phenomenon.

State the Author's Claim (the Hypothesis)

The first step in any scientific experiment is to state the hypothesis. The researcher then devises an experiment that will test whether the hypothesis is true. The articles in this anthology make at least one claim about alien abductions that can be quickly summarized by the article's title. To evaluate the articles in this anthology, make a table listing the major claim of each article.

Author	Hypothesis
John E. Mack	All alien abductions are the same.
Scott Corrales	Claims of alien abductions occur all over the world.
David M. Jacobs	
Budd Hopkins	
Bill Chalker	Kary Mullis was abducted by aliens.
Michael Shermer	People who claim to have been abducted by aliens hallucinated their experiences.
Joe Nickell	
Robert A. Baker	
Robert E. Bartholomew and George S. Howard	Alien abduction stories are the result of fanciful imaginations.
Jim Giglio and Scott Snell	There is no evidence that aliens have visited Earth.

A hypothesis should be written as a clear, specific, and provable statement. Chalker's hypothesis, "Kary Mullis was abducted by aliens," seems to be clear and specific, but in reality, it is not. Mullis saw a talking raccoon in the woods and then blacked out for several hours. A better hypothesis would specify exactly what the author's main point is:

| Bill Chalker | Kary Mullis had an unusual experience in the woods. |

Now analyze the hypothesis of the article by John E. Mack. Readers should consider whether an author can claim that "all," or even most, experiences are the same. This hypothesis should be changed to a more provable statement. Read Mack's article and restate his hypothesis.

John E. Mack	

Some articles may not even have a hypothesis; if the article is strictly the author's opinion, it may lack a provable statement. On the other hand, some authors may make more than one claim in their article; if so, they will have more than one hypothesis.

Hypotheses are not listed for four articles in the long table above. Read the articles and write a clear, specific, and provable statement of the author's claim for each of these articles.

Gather the Author's Evidence Supporting the Claim

Once the author's hypothesis has been determined, the next step is to list his or her supporting evidence. While neither Chalker nor Mullis actually say that Mullis was abducted by aliens, that is their conclusion after they analyze the facts surrounding that particular evening.

1. Mullis was walking to his outhouse when he met a glowing raccoon who spoke to him.
2. Mullis was not under the influence of drugs or alcohol because he had driven a very windy road without mishap to his cabin in the mountains.
3. Mullis does not remember anything else about the evening until many hours later, when he found himself walking on a road far from where he last remembered being.

4. Mullis's clothes were dry, so he had not spent the night outside.

5. Mullis's flashlight was missing and never found.

6. The groceries were still on the floor of Mullis's cabin, where he had left them before going to the outhouse.

7. Mullis later developed an irrational fear of a particular area of woods on his property.

8. On another occasion, Mullis's daughter also disappeared for several hours at the cabin and reappeared on the same stretch of road where Mullis found himself.

9. Mullis saw a book about an alien abduction and the cover illustration of an alien and the story seemed instantly familiar to him. His daughter called him to tell him to buy the book and to tell him of her experience in the woods.

10. A friend—who was ignorant of Mullis's glowing raccoon story—encountered a glowing man one evening at the cabin and later found himself outside his hotel room without knowing how he got there.

Examine the Evidence Used to Support the Claim

Among the different kinds of evidence used to support a claim are eyewitness testimony, such as that used by Mullis, and statements of fact. Physical evidence is usually some sort of proof or evidence that can be held or examined. When analyzing an author's claims, it is important to differentiate between a factual truth that has been verified and an author's unverified claims of fact.

Eyewitness Testimony

Eyewitness testimony is a personal account of what someone saw. If there were no other witnesses, the testimony may not be able to be independently verified. Eyewitness testimony is the most common form of evidence used in re-search about alien abductions simply because there is little or no physical evidence available. Chalker uses his entire article to tell what Kary Mullis, his daughter, and a friend saw; therefore, it is an excellent example of eyewitness testi-mony. Chalker offers a lot of information about what Mullis saw and experienced, but readers must always keep in mind that eyewitnesses are notoriously unreliable in re-porting what actually happened. If five people witness an event, such as an abduction, there are likely to be five dif-ferent interpretations of what happened, what the aliens looked like, how long the event lasted, and so forth. Be-cause memory tends to change details here and there, the most reliable reports come from those witnesses who im-mediately write down what they saw.

Researchers who study alien abductions consider not only the first-person accounts of the abduction but also the reputation of the person telling the story. Some people claim to have been abducted by aliens as a ploy for getting publicity or fame, whereas other abductees shun publicity for fear of being ridiculed. Researchers also consider whether the witnesses are responsible, reliable, and honest in their everyday lives. Mullis is an esteemed scientist who is used to examining and analyzing evidence to ensure that his results are accurate. However, some of his peers consider him a "maverick thinker" because some of his ideas and theories are a little unusual. It should be considered, though, that his "maverick" thinking probably contributed to his winning the Nobel Prize. In addition, Mullis's auto-biography for the Nobel Prize committee tells a story about how he chatted and drank beers with his maternal grandfa-ther's ghost for a few days after his grandfather's death. Many people would have a hard time accepting the veracity of such a story.

Statements of Fact

Many times the author will present information as a statement of fact when, in actuality, there is no way to verify that
the information is true. For example, Chalker quotes Mullis
as stating that he saw a glowing raccoon that talked to him,
but he has no independent witnesses, photographs, videotape, or any other corroborating evidence to substantiate his
claim. However, the fact that two other people—who claim
to have had no prior knowledge of Mullis encountering a
glowing and talking raccoon—had similar experiences on
Mullis's property may support his claims of encountering
an alien. Of the items listed on his evidence list, which
statements can be verified as true and which cannot?

Consider Alternative Hypotheses

One of the most important steps in analyzing evidence is determining if there are other logical explanations that could
explain what the witness saw or experienced. For example,
many sightings of unidentified flying objects (UFOs, or alien
spaceships) have been identified by ufologists as sightings of
the moon, stars, satellites, weather balloons, or airplanes. According to Chalker, Mullis contends that the talking raccoon
was real and not a drunken hallucination because Mullis
was not drunk. Mullis's claim that he had driven a difficult
road does not offer sufficient proof of sobriety, however.
People under the influence of alcohol and drugs have been
known to successfully accomplish difficult tasks without
mishap. Consider the statements of fact listed for Mullis; are
there any other plausible explanations for what he said he
saw and experienced other than an abduction by aliens?

Draw a Conclusion About the Author's Claim

Readers should now have a list of items that support the author's claim and refute it. Just because one side may have

more items listed, however, does not necessarily mean that the truth belongs on that side; some evidence is more important and should be given more weight when making a decision. In some cases, a person's reputation may have more weight than the lack of corroboration, but the opposite may hold true as well. What do you think? Has Mullis presented enough evidence to support his claim that he was abducted by aliens?

Michael Shermer's Explanation: Hallucination

Professional debunker Michael Shermer has an alternative theory for alien abduction experiences:

Michael Shermer	People who claim to have been abducted by aliens hallucinated their experiences.

Shermer's reputation is also impressive. He is director of the Skeptics Society and has proven that many claims about paranormal phenomena are either deliberate hoaxes or normal events that have been innocently mistaken for something unusual. In his article in this anthology, Shermer explains how many "abductees" could really be hallucinating their experiences. To support this claim, he discusses an experience he had in which he believed aliens were impersonating his road crew during a long bicycle race.

Gather the Author's Evidence

1. The author experienced much pressure to do well during a long bicycle race.
2. The author got little sleep in the early stages of the race.
3. During the race, he believed space aliens abducted his road crew.

4. The aliens then returned in the bodies of his road crew with the intent of killing him.
5. The author knew that the members of his road crew were actually space aliens.
6. Despite the author's intensive questioning, the aliens knew the most obscure facts about the crew members' lives.
7. The aliens forced the author to take a short nap.
8. After getting some much-needed rest, the author realized that he had hallucinated the encounter with aliens due to stress and a lack of sleep.
9. Other "alien abductions" are also undoubtedly the result of altered states and unusual circumstances.
10. Therefore, it is more likely that there are other, more logical explanations for unusual experiences than that of alien abduction.

Examine the Evidence

Shermer's article is a variation on the theme of alien abduction, using his own experience to generalize about the experiences of others. His article is not meant to be an in-depth examination of alien abductions; rather, it presents an alternative hypothesis for the phenomena. Shermer uses generalizations, statements of fact, and bias to support his argument.

Generalizations

Authors often use generalizations—explicit or implied, which may be either true or false—in the hope that their readers will make their own generalizations. For example, Shermer offers his personal experience of hallucinating an alien abduction. He wants his readers to generalize that most people's claims of alien abduction are like his—caused by an altered state of consciousness due to stress, a lack of sleep, or some other factor.

Statements of Fact

Reread Shermer's article and determine what his statements of fact are and whether they can actually be proven.

Personal Opinion or Bias

Shermer states clearly at the beginning of his article that he is a skeptic and believes that there are other explanations for claims of alien abduction. Does his bias influence your assessment of his article?

Consider Alternative Hypotheses

Shermer does consider that perhaps people truly are being abducted by aliens, but he argues that the most logical explanation—altered states of consciousness—is the much more likely one. Is his reasoning valid? Are there other alternatives he should be considering?

Draw a Conclusion

Consider the evidence presented by Shermer. Which author—Mullis or Shermer—makes the strongest case about alien abductions?

Other Kinds of Evidence

Some writers try to influence their readers by including the views of celebrities or experts in their argument. Although celebrities may not be well informed on a topic, some readers are convinced of a claim's truthfulness if they read that somebody famous endorses such a view. However, celebrity endorsements usually provide little solid evidence that can be used to prove or disprove a claim.

On the other hand, including opinions from scientists, researchers, and other experts is a valuable tactic that can provide necessary information that a reader needs to make an informed decision. The reader should be informed of the expert's qualifications, and the expert cited should have some relevance to the question at hand. For example, ufologists and doctors can give their opinion about whether physical marks on abductees' bodies or metal objects found under their skin are really signs of medical experimentation by aliens or are from some other source. However, medical doctors probably are not the best experts to use to discuss other evidence, such as whether a UFO is actually a spaceship or a star, planet, or satellite.

Other experts in the field of alien abduction include hypnotists. Many people do not consciously remember their abductions. Like Mullis, they know that something strange has happened to them, but they do not remember exactly what. Some people realize that several hours have passed without their being aware of it, and others find scars or other marks on their bodies that they have no recollection of ever receiving. Counselors and therapists sometimes use hypnosis to discover details about an event that the witness does not consciously remember. Other hypnotists can study the transcripts of the sessions and determine whether the hypnotist asked the subject leading questions to get the desired answer.

Statistical Evidence

A poll sponsored by ufologists Budd Hopkins and David M. Jacobs in 1991 estimated that nearly 4 million Americans (about 2 percent of the population) had been abducted by aliens. This claim is disputed by skeptics, who question the methods used to determine the number of abductees. More people appear to believe in the existence of aliens, though; a 1996 Gallup poll reports that 72 percent of Americans believe there is life beyond Earth. However, just because people believe in extraterrestrial life does NOT mean that aliens have visited Earth and abducted humans for scientific experiments.

When considering statistical evidence, it is important to know who collected the information and how long ago it was done. Polls conducted by groups other than independent polling organizations such as Gallup or news groups sometimes have biased questions that lead to the desired result. For example, whereas independent organizations are more likely to ask people if they have been abducted by aliens, a group that believes in alien abduction might ask if the respondents have experienced any of the common signs of alien abductions—episodes of "missing time," scars on their bodies they do not remember receiving—and then infer that the respondents have been abducted because they answered *yes* to the questions.

Physical Evidence

Sometimes abductees claim they have physical evidence that proves they were abducted by aliens: "scoop marks" or other injuries or scars on their bodies; strange objects inserted under their skin for tracking them; burn marks or other signs from the spaceship at the site of the abduction; or photographs of the craft. These claims of physical evidence must be studied by investigators who are trained in collecting and analyzing such evidence and determining whether such evidence is real or faked. When discussing physical evidence in their articles, authors should explain the process through which the evidence was determined to be real, a hoax, or inconclusive.

Weighing the Evidence

It is difficult to determine whether people actually have been abducted by aliens. Abductees truly believe they have been taken by aliens into spaceships against their will, examined, perhaps even forced to suffer invasive medical procedures, and then returned to their homes with hours missing from their memories. Yet science seems to contradict the very premise of alien abduction. Readers researching alien abduction should keep in mind the author's qualifications. The views of a writer who is prominent in the field of ufology or skepticism can be taken more seriously than an author who has no experience in the field and is just reporting an investigation by someone else. Readers should also consider an author's bias toward the subject; a writer who includes—and counters—objections to the views being discussed may be more trustworthy than a writer who totally ignores the other side of the argument. Likewise, an author who provides and documents evidence—such as it may be—to support his or her contention may be more credible than an author who does not.

In addition, readers should examine the way the article is written. One author may present his or her opinions as fact without evidence to support them, another may clearly indicate that the article is purely conjecture or opinion, and yet a third may offer only documented facts and draw a conclusion from those facts. Some authors may try to write their articles factually but provide little specific evidence to support their conclusion. Even articles that are written in a factual manner may not in truth be factual. For example, the statement "I was abducted by aliens" is a factual statement, but it is not a true statement since it cannot be independently verified. Similarly, the statement "Aliens have not visited Earth" is factual, but it is impossible to prove its veracity.

Readers trying to determine whether claims of alien abduction are true must consider the fact that a large percentage of abductees have fantasy-prone personalities (meaning they have fantasies that they believe are real) and sometimes confabulate during hypnosis. However, skeptical arguments are not always legitimate either. Some reports of alien abduction can be proven to be hoaxes, but others cannot. Those that are proven to be hoaxes generally deviate from the norm regarding sequence of the abduction, how the aliens appeared, and what happened during the abduction. Some abduction reports are influenced by the media—popular movies and books and accounts that detail what the aliens looked like, among other things—but in some cases, children too young to have been influenced by the media and popular culture have also reported being abducted by aliens.

What Do You Think?

Choose and study an article in this anthology that has not been discussed in this analysis. Evaluate the author's arguments according to the criteria discussed in this section, including the author's credibility, the evidence presented, eyewitness testimony, author bias, and statements of fact.

Name of article_____ Author_____

1. State the author's hypothesis.

2. List the evidence.

3. Examine the evidence. For each item listed under evidence, state what type of evidence it is (eyewitness testimony, statement of fact, etc.) and evaluate it. Does it appear to be valid evidence? Does it appear to support the author's hypothesis?

4. Consider alternative hypotheses. Does the author examine other explanations? Is the author fair in his or her acceptance or rejection of the alternatives? Are the author's conclusions about other hypotheses reasonable? Does the author ignore alternatives you believe should be considered?

5. Decide how reliable you think the article's conclusion is. Is the author's conclusion adequately supported by the evidence presented? Do you agree with the author's conclusion? List the reasons for your decision.

Now choose another article to analyze, but this time select one in which you have a personal opinion concerning the veracity of the conclusion. Ignore your bias of the article and examine it using the criteria mentioned above. Does your opinion of the article change? Explain.

Do not be surprised if, after reading articles that both support and criticize alien abduction, you still are undecided about whether people are being abducted by aliens. Researchers have been arguing about alien abduction for more than thirty years and still have not reached a consensus about the reality of the phenomenon.

Appendix

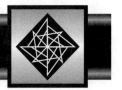

Have You Been Abducted by an Alien?

Jason Nicholls

Many people who have been abducted by aliens do not remember the experience because aliens are believed to be able to erase people's memories or replace them with false memories. Some abductees attribute their strange memories or feelings to dreams without realizing they have been abducted. However, abductees share many common experiences. By taking a short quiz, people can determine whether it is likely that they have been abducted by aliens. Jason Nicholls is a reporter for the London-based newspaper *Sunday People*.

D o you have the secret feeling you may be special or chosen? Are there times you find it hard to sleep at night? Have you ever woken up with a nosebleed, or found blood on your pillow in the morning?

As strange as it may seem, not only could these incidents be connected but they could also be evidence of a more sinister force.

According to an American professor they are just some of the symptoms experienced by people who have been abducted by aliens.

An Abduction Survey

Now Dr Marilyn Ruben, who runs Michigan University's Alien Abduction Experience and Research Centre, has devised a 25-question survey to help YOU discover whether you've been abducted.

Dr Ruben, who runs the centre with her husband Daniel, a fellow UFO expert, says: "People don't realise they have been abducted because it's said that the aliens are able to wipe their memories.

"But while it's believed they are able to wipe any memory of the abduction away, they're not, for example, able to replace the time that was lost.

"We aimed to show people that experiences they may dismiss out of hand and put down to drinking too much on a Saturday night could in fact be evidence pointing to the fact that they have been abducted.

"The kind of feelings or experiences I'm talking about are where you feel you may be psychic, have dreams you are flying, or have trouble sleeping through the night for unexplained reasons."

Before beginning their research, the Rubens spent a year interviewing people who claimed to be alien abductees. "We wanted a clear picture of the experiences these people were having," said Dr Ruben.

"What we found was that a huge number of people in the USA believe they have been abducted.

"This can come from something as simple as losing track

of time, to discovering something has been implanted in your body.

"People who had been having routine dental checks or medical scans were also discovering things in their bodies which they didn't realise were there. More importantly they didn't know how they got there.

"Once we had completed the initial stages, we then sat down and devised the questions. Our aim was to come up with questions where the person answering them could not be influenced in any way."

The Rubens believe there are thousands of people across the world being abducted on a regular basis.

"We want to make the world aware there is life out there. We want people to know we are not alone. And that those visiting us have far more power than we do."

To help their research Dr Ruben has put her questionnaire out on the Internet (www.abduct.com).

More than 4,000 people have responded from Britain alone and Dr Ruben says that 20 per cent discovered they had been abducted. To test whether you've been visited by little green men from Mars but have no memory of it, the *Sunday People* has reproduced the questionaire.

Just Answer These Questions

1. Do you take more vitamins than most people? Yes/No
2. Do you have sinus trouble or migraine headaches? Yes/No
3. Do you feel you might be psychic? Yes/No
4. Do you secretly feel you are special or chosen? Yes/No
5. Do you secretly fear being accosted or kidnapped if you do not constantly monitor your surroundings? Yes/No
6. Do you have trouble sleeping through the night? Yes/No

7. Have you thought about installing a security system in your home? Yes/No

8. Do you have dreams of flying or being outside your body? Yes/No

9. Do you dream about seeing or being inside UFOs? Yes/No

10. As a child or teenager, was there a place you secretly believed held a spiritual meaning for you? Yes/No

11. As a child or adult, do or did you hear voices talking to you? Yes/No

12. Have you ever experienced a period of time, while awake, where you could not remember what you did during that period of time? Yes/No

13. Have you ever seen faces near your bed which you could not explain? Yes/No

14. Have you ever seen a UFO from a distance? Yes/No

15. Have you ever seen a UFO up close? Yes/No

16. If you have seen a UFO, either from a distance or close, were you compelled to be near it? Yes/No

17. Do you have a waking memory of being inside a UFO? Yes/No

18. Does talk of aliens upset you? Yes/No

19. Have you had multiple UFO sightings? Yes/No

20. Are you sensitive to issues affecting the earth? Yes/No

21. Do you dream angels are telling you about mankind? Yes/No

22. Does your home have unexplainable sounds which you attribute to ghosts? Yes/No

23. Have you had nosebleeds or found blood stains on your pillow in the morning? Yes/No

24. Have X-rays ever found strange objects in your body? Yes/No

25. Have you woken to find strange marks or bruises on your body? Yes/No

Just answer yes or no to the questions.

Count the number of "Yes" answers, and then check your scores below.

Results

0–5 "Yes" answers: Don't worry. You have not been abducted.

6–10 "Yes" answers: You have a lot of shared experiences with alien abductees but have probably not been abducted yourself.

11–15 "Yes" answers: There's a strong possibility you have been abducted. You share so many common experiences with those who claim to be abductees that you should explore this further.

16–20 "Yes" answers: You have been abducted by aliens but until now you probably won't have realised it.

21–25 "Yes" answers: You are definitely an alien abductee. You may well have suspected this before. You should think about ways to protect yourself from such abductions in the future.

The Meaning Behind This Strange Quiz

At first reading many of the University questions contained in the survey seem to have no connection to alien abductions.

Dr Marilyn Ruben explains: "It was quite deliberate. The way the questions are phrased is not meant to influence the way people answer them.

"But, what may seem like a simple question, can have a far deeper meaning, depending on how you answer it. And what might seem like a question totally unconnected to aliens can actually be quite relevant.

"For example, we ask about bruises on the body because people who have been abducted often say they had bruises from being manhandled by the aliens.

"Blood stains and nosebleeds are relevant because abductees who remember tests having been performed on them, often find blood on their pillows."

Dr Ruben says headaches and sinus troubles can be linked to objects placed inside the brains of abductees.

Other questions are devised to discover whether people have been brainwashed by their captors.

Dr Ruben explains: "The question about the environment has been put in because alien abductees say they receive a huge amount of instruction on how to care for the planet."

Although not having direct memories of being captured, many abductees start to behave and think slightly differently.

"That's why we ask whether people have thought about installing a security system in their homes," she says.

"While consciously people may not be aware they are being abducted, deep down they may know.

"If people have fitted an alarm in their home, on a very subconscious level this could point to the fact they are trying to protect themselves from being taken again."

But there is one question that Dr Ruben admits may not be an entirely accurate guide.

"It's very common for abductees to experience a period of time while awake where they could not remember what they did during that period of time.

"It might mean they've been with aliens—but it can also happen for a number of more mundane reasons," she admits.

Organizations to Contact

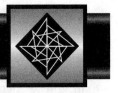

The editors have compiled the following list of organizations concerned with the issues debated in this book. The descriptions are derived from materials provided by the organizations. All have publications or information available for interested readers. The list was compiled on the date of publication of the present volume; the information provided here may change. Be aware that many organizations take several weeks or longer to respond to inquiries, so allow as much time as possible.

Center for the Study of Extraterrestrial Intelligence (CSETI)
PO Box 265, Crozet, VA 22932-0265
(301) 249-3915
website: www.cseti.org

CSETI is a nonprofit research and educational organization that is dedicated to establishing peaceful and sustainable contact with extraterrestrial life-forms. Its goal is to establish contact with and educate society about extraterrestrial intelligence. The center publishes numerous position papers and field reports on UFOs.

Citizens Against UFO Secrecy, Inc. (CAUS)
PO Box 20351, Sedona, AZ 86341-0351
(602) 818-8248
website: www.caus.org

CAUS is a nonprofit public interest group that believes that extraterrestrial intelligence is in contact with Earth and that there is a campaign of secrecy to conceal this knowledge. Its goals are to educate and enlighten the public about this cover-up and to fund further research into extraterrestrial contact with Earth.

Committee for the Scientific Investigation of Claims of the Paranormal (CSICOP)
PO Box 703, Amherst, NY 14226
(716) 636-1425 • fax: (716) 636-1733
e-mail: info@csicop.org • website: www.csicop.org

Established in 1976, the committee is a nonprofit scientific and educational organization that encourages the critical investigation of paranormal and fringe-science claims from a scientific point of view. It disseminates factual information about the results of such inquiries to the scientific community and the public. CSICOP publishes *Skeptical Inquirer* magazine, the children's book *Bringing UFOs Down to Earth*, and bibliographies of other published materials that examine claims of the paranormal.

Federal Bureau of Investigation (FBI)
Headquarters, J. Edgar Hoover Building
935 Pennsylvania Ave. NW, Washington, DC 20535-0001
(202) 324-3000
website: www.fbi.gov

The FBI hosts an official website that includes, among other things, an electronic reading room. The reading room offers all published FBI findings and articles on UFOs, with such topics as "Animal/Cattle Mutilation" and "Roswell."

J. Allen Hynek Center for UFO Studies (CUFOS)
2457 W. Peterson Ave., Chicago, IL 60659
(773) 271-3611
e-mail: infocenter@cufos.org • website: www.cufos.org

CUFOS is a nonprofit scientific organization dedicated to the continuing examination and analysis of the UFO phenomenon. The center acts as a clearinghouse for the reporting and researching of UFO experiences. It publishes the quarterly *International UFO Reporter*, the *Journal of UFO Studies*, monographs, and special reports.

Mutual UFO Network (MUFON)
PO Box 369, Morrison, CO 80465-0369
website: www.mufon.com

The Mutual UFO Network is one of the oldest and largest organizations that studies and investigates reports of UFO sightings. It maintains a worldwide UFO database which provides up-to-date reports of sightings by date; state in which the UFO was sighted; and UFO shape, size, color, and flight characteristics. It publishes the *MUFON UFO Journal* and an annual collection of *Symposium Proceedings*.

National UFO Reporting Center
PO Box 45623, University Station, Seattle, WA 98145
(206) 722-3000
website: www.ufocenter.com

Founded in 1974, the center serves as a headquarters for reporting possible UFO sightings. Such reports are recorded and disseminated for objective research and information purposes. The center maintains an online database of all reports and also publishes a monthly newsletter.

SETI League
PO Box 555, Little Ferry, NJ 07643
(201) 641-1770 • fax: (201) 641-1771
e-mail: info@setileague.org • website: www.setileague.org

The SETI League is a membership-supported, nonprofit educational and scientific organization dedicated to the search for extraterrestrial intelligence. Its publications include the books *Project Cyclops* and the *SETI League Technical Manual* as well as the quarterly newsletter *SearchLites*.

Skeptics Society
PO Box 338, Altadena, CA 91001
(818) 794-3119 • fax: (818) 794-1301
e-mail: skepticmag@aol.com • website: www.skeptic.com

The society is composed of scholars, scientists, and historians who promote the use of scientific methods to scrutinize such nonscientific beliefs as religion, superstition, mysticism, and New Age beliefs. It is devoted to the investigation of extraordinary claims and revolutionary ideas and to the promotion of science and critical thinking. The society publishes the quarterly *Skeptic Magazine*.

Society for Scientific Exploration (SSE)
PO Box 3818, Charlottesville, VA 22903
(804) 924-4905
website: www.scientificexploration.org

Affiliated with the University of Virginia's Department of Astronomy, the society seeks to provide a professional forum for presentations, criticisms, and debates concerning topics that are ignored or given inadequate study by mainstream academia. It strives to increase understanding of the factors that at present limit the scope of scientific inquiry. The society publishes the quarterlies *Journal of Scientific Exploration* and *Explorer.*

Ufomind
PO Box 81166, Las Vegas, NV 89103
(702) 227-1818 • fax: (702) 227-1816
website: www.ufomind.com

Ufomind hosts the world's most extensive website on UFOs and paranormal phenomena, and it seeks to provide a forum where all sides can be heard on these issues. The website houses a research index and a bookstore.

For Further Research

Books

Joel Achenbach, *Captured by Aliens: The Search for Life and Truth in a Very Large Universe.* New York: Simon and Schuster, 1999.

Robert E. Bartholomew and George S. Howard, *UFOs and Alien Contact: Two Centuries of Mystery.* Amherst, NY: Prometheus, 1998.

William J. Birnes and Harold Burt, *Unsolved UFO Mysteries: The World's Most Compelling Cases of Alien Encounter.* New York: Warner, 2000.

Peter A. Campbell, *Alien Encounters.* Brookfield, CT: Millbrook Press, 2000.

Dolores Cannon, *The Custodians: "Beyond Abduction."* Huntsville, AR: Ozark Mountain Publishing, 1999.

Jerome Clark, *The UFO Book: Encyclopedia of the Extraterrestrial.* Detroit, MI: Visible Ink Press, 1998.

David Darling, *The Extraterrestrial Encyclopedia: An Alphabetical Reference to All Life in the Universe.* New York: Three Rivers Press, 2000.

Preston Dennett, *Extraterrestrial Visitations: True Accounts of Contact.* St. Paul: Llewellyn, 2001.

Hilary Evans, *From Other Worlds: Aliens, Abductions and UFOs.* Pleasantville, NY: Readers Digest, 1998.

Bill Fawcett, ed., *Making Contact: A Serious Handbook for Locating and Communicating with Extraterrestrials.* New York: William Morrow, 1997.

Richard F. Haines, *CE-5: Close Encounters of the Fifth Kind.* Naperville, IL: Sourcebooks, 1999.

David M. Jacobs, *The Threat.* New York: Simon and Schuster, 1998.

David M. Jacobs, ed., *UFOs and Abductions: Challenging the Borders of Knowledge.* Lawrence: University Press of Kansas, 2000.

Michael Kurland, *The Complete Idiot's Guide to Extraterrestrial Intelligence.* New York: Alpha Books, 1999.

John E. Mack, *Passport to the Cosmos: Human Transformation and Alien Encounters.* New York: Crown, 1999.

Jim Marrs, *Alien Agenda: Investigating the Extraterrestrials Among Us.* New York: HarperCollins, 1997.

Kary Mullis, *Dancing Naked in the Mind Field.* New York: Pantheon, 1998.

Phil Patton, *Dreamland: Travels Inside the Secret World of Roswell and Area 51.* New York: Villard, 1998.

Kevin D. Randle, Russ Estes, and William P. Cone, *The Abduction Enigma: The Truth Behind the Mass Alien Abductions of the Late Twentieth Century.* New York: Forge, 1999.

Rudy Rucker, *Saucer Wisdom.* New York: Forge, 1999.

Peter A. Sturrock, *The UFO Enigma: A New Review of the Physical Evidence.* New York: Warner, 1999.

Susan Wright, *UFO Headquarters: Investigations on Current Extraterrestrial Activity.* New York: St. Martin's Press, 1998.

Periodicals

Robert A. Baker, "The Alien Abduction Puzzle: Solved!" *Skeptical Inquirer,* January 2000.

Thomas E. Bullard, "Abductions and Researcher Bias: How to Lose Your Way," *International UFO Reporter*, Spring 1999.

Julia Duin, "If the Truth Is Out There, the Feds Aren't Telling," *Insight on the News*, May 18, 1998.

Julia Duin, "Space Aliens Steal Kisses?" *Insight on the News*, August 9, 1999.

Cynthia Fox, "The Search for Extraterrestrial Life," *New York*, March 2000.

Bruce Goldberg, "Hypnotic Highways," *Fate*, February 1999.

Mark Goldblatt, "Aliens in America," *Reason*, March 1999.

Matthew Graber, "Beware the Dark Side," *Fate*, May 2002.

Jim Keith, "Roswell UFO Bombshell," *Fate*, January 2000.

Susan McClelland, "UFOs . . . Seriously," *Mclean's*, August 13, 2001.

Samuel McCracken, "Close Encounters of the Harvard Kind," *Commentary*, March 2000.

Hans S. Nichols, "Clones of Aliens Are Among Us?" *Insight on the News*, October 29, 2001.

Joe Nickell, "Alien Implants: The New 'Hard Evidence,'" *Skeptical Inquirer*, September–October 1998.

Andrew D. Reisner, "A Psychological Case Study of 'Demon' and 'Alien' Visitation," *Skeptical Inquirer*, March 2001.

Vladimir V. Rubtsov, "Domes of Wrath," *Fate*, April 2002.

Jim Wilson, "When UFOs Land," *Popular Mechanics*, May 2001.

Index

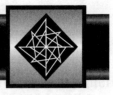